A BREATH OF FRESH AIR

CELEBRATING NATURE AND SCHOOL GARDENS

A BREATH OF FRESH AIR

CELEBRATING NATURE AND SCHOOL GARDENS

ELISE HOUGHTON

PHOTOGRAPHY BY
ROBERT CHRISTIE

WITH A FOREWORD BY
MARGARET ATWOOD

THE LEARNXS FOUNDATION *&* SUMACH PRESS
IN CO-OPERATION WITH THE
TORONTO DISTRICT SCHOOL BOARD

NATIONAL LIBRARY OF CANADA CATALOGUING IN PUBLICATION DATA

Houghton, Elise
  A breath of fresh air: celebrating nature and school gardens/Elise Houghton.

Co-published by Sumach Press.
Includes bibliographical references.
ISBN 0-920020-61-5

1. School gardens—Ontario. 2. School gardens—Case
studies. 3. Outdoor education—Case studies. 4. School grounds.
I. Learnxs Foundation. II. Titles.

SB56.T67H68 2003   635'.071'0713541   C2003-900530-5

Edited by Beth McAuley & Rhea Tregebov
Designed by Elizabeth Martin

Printed and bound in Canada

Project development team:
CETA RAMKHALAWANSINGH
RICHARD CHRISTIE
DONALD NETHERY
ELIZABETH MARTIN

LEARNXS FOUNDATION
5050 Yonge Street
Toronto Ontario
M2N 5N8

SUMACH PRESS
1415 Bathurst Street #202
Toronto Ontario
M5R 3H8

TORONTO DISTRICT SCHOOL BOARD
5050 Yonge Street
Toronto Ontario
M2N 5N8

CONTENTS

PREFACE

A Breath of Fresh Air celebrates the learning that takes place in outdoor classrooms. More than ever before we need to understand how to live with nature and what we must do to keep the earth fit for future generations.

Our goal is to nurture a school system in which our students achieve ecological literacy in the classroom, in the school yard and in the wilderness. When learning takes place in a diversity of settings using a variety of approaches, we are more likely to achieve success in building sustainable communities.

This book, which grew out of the planning process for the millennium celebrations, documents the remarkable efforts made by students, staff, parents, volunteers and various donors. At the outset the project was sponsored by the Toronto District School Board and the Learnxs Foundation. We are indebted to Margaret Atwood, Rob Christie, Elise Houghton and Elizabeth Martin for their creative contribution to this book.

It is our sincere hope that the images and stories in these pages convince you to play your part along with our students in celebrating and conserving nature.

Trustee Donna Cansfield
CO-CHAIR
TORONTO DISTRICT SCHOOL BOARD

Trustee Shelley Carroll
CO-CHAIR
TORONTO DISTRICT SCHOOL BOARD

Ceta Ramkhalawansingh
PRESIDENT
LEARNXS FOUNDATION

David Reid
DIRECTOR OF EDUCATION
TORONTO DISTRICT SCHOOL BOARD

Toronto, Canada
Spring 2003

*I believe we are at a crossroads now as far as environmental responsibility
is concerned. Each and every one of us must begin to take care and do
whatever we can to keep the earth fit for our own and future generations.
I hope that by having students involved in gardening and managing the
natural surroundings, they will develop a love of the outdoors and a desire
to maintain green spaces even in highly populated urban centres.*

SHARON MAISONVILLE,
TEACHER, TERRAVIEW-WILLOWFIELD PUBLIC SCHOOL,
TORONTO DISTRICT SCHOOL BOARD

*Learning in the school garden is learning in the real world at its very
best. It is beneficial for the development of the individual student and the
school community, and it is one of the best ways for children to become
ecologically literate and thus able to contribute to building
a sustainable future.*

FRITJOF CAPRA,
ECOLITERACY: THE CHALLENGE FOR EDUCATION IN THE NEXT CENTURY

*If I were to choose only one lesson, one gift to give to the young,
it would be to inspire in them a reverence for life, and an awareness
of the interconnectedness of all living beings and
the earth that is our home.*

DONNA HAVINGA,
ECOLOGICAL RESTORATION CONSULTANT

FOREWORD

BY MARGARET ATWOOD

VICTORY GARDENS

I

WHEN I WAS SMALL, people had Victory Gardens. This was during the Second World War, and the idea was that if people grew their own vegetables, then the food produced by the farmers would be freed up for use by the army. There was another strong motivator: rationing was in effect for things you were unlikely to be able to grow yourself, such as sugar, butter, milk, tea, cheese and meat, so the more you could grow, the better you would eat, and the better the soldiers would eat, too. Thus, by digging and hoeing and weeding and watering, you too could help win the war.

But people did not live on vegetables and fruit alone. Anything resembling protein or fat was precious. Shortening, margarine and bacon drippings were cherished; gizzards, livers, feet and necks were not scorned. Bits and scraps that today would be carelessly tossed into the trash were hoarded and treasured, making their way from their first appearance as, say, a roasted chicken, through various other incarnations as noodle-and-leftovers casseroles, soups and stews, and mystery ingredients in pot pies. A housewife's skill was measured by the number of times she could serve up the same thing without your knowing it.

Careful planning was required; waste was frowned on. This meant that everything, not only from such things as chickens but from the garden, had to be used, and, if

necessary, preserved. Home freezing hadn't arrived yet, so canning and preserving were major activities, especially in the late summer, when the garden would produce more than the family could eat. Housewives cooked up vast quantities of tomato sauce, pickles, green beans, strawberries, apple-sauce — vegetables and fruits of all kinds. These would be eaten in the winter, along with the cabbages and the winter squash and the root vegetables — beets, carrots, turnips and potatoes — that had been stored in a cool place.

As children growing up in this era, we knew that every seedling was precious. We were part of the system: we weeded and watered, we picked off cabbage worms and tomato worms and potato bugs. We dug peelings and cores and husks back into the soil; we fended off woodchucks; we sprinkled wood ashes. If lucky enough to be near a source of blueberries, we picked them; and we picked peas and beans, and we dug potatoes. I can't claim that all of this was spontaneous labour, joyfully performed: such tasks were chores. But the connection between tending the vegetables and eating the results was clear. Food did not come wrapped in plastic from the supermarket — there were hardly any supermarkets, anyway. It came out of the ground or it grew on a bush or tree, and it needed water and sunlight and proper fertilization.

My mother's generation was brought up strictly: children were expected to finish everything on their plates, whether they liked it or not, and if they failed to do this they were made to sit at the dinner table until they did. Frequently they were told to remember other children who were starving — the Armenians, the Chinese. I used to think this was both harsh — why force a child to eat when it wasn't hungry? — and ridiculous — what good would eating your bread crusts do for the Armenians? But this method doubtless had at its heart an insistence on respect. Many people had laboured to produce the food on the plate, among them the parents, who had either grown it or paid hard-earned cash for it. You could not snub this food. You should show a proper gratitude. Hence the once-widespread practice of saying grace at meals, which has fallen into disuse. Why be grateful for something — now — so easy to come by?

II

In the plotline of life on earth, gardens are a recent twist. They date back to perhaps ten thousand years ago, when the gathering and hunting that had been the prevailing model for 99 percent of human history could no longer sustain societies in the face of diminishing game and wild food supplies.

When the total population of the earth was less than four million people — before, the experts estimate, about ten thousand years ago — the gathering and hunting way of life was still viable. The myth of the Golden Age appears to have some foundation in fact: food was there in the wild, for the taking, and people didn't have to spend much of their time obtaining it. After that point, conditions became harder, as communities had to adapt more labour-intensive stratagems to feed themselves. "Agriculture" is sometimes used to denote any form of cultivation or domestication — of herd animals for meat and milk, of garden crops and fruit trees, of field crops such as wheat and barley. Sometimes a distinction is made between "agriculture," in which large areas are farmed using the plough to break the ground — traditionally a male activity — and "horticulture," in which smaller, individual garden plots are cultivated, traditionally by women. "Horticulture" is thought to have come first, but all agree that there was a long period of transition in which gathering and hunting, horticulture and agriculture, existed side by side.

Many ills have been ascribed to agriculture. In gathering and hunting cultures, food was — as a rule — obtained and eaten as needed. But once agriculture became firmly established — once crops could be harvested and stored, once surpluses could be accumulated, and, not incidentally, transported, exchanged, destroyed, and stolen — social strata became possible, with slaves at the lower end, peasants above them, and a ruling class on top that made no physical effort in order to eat. Armies could march on surplus food supplies; religious hierarchies could tithe; kings could preside; taxes could be levied. Crop monocultures became widespread, with a dependence on only a few kinds of food, resulting not only in malnutrition, but in famine at times of crop failure.

A city-dweller's relation to food is — as a system — closer to the gathering-hunting model than to the horticultural-agricultural one. You don't grow the food yourself, or raise it in the form of an animal. Instead you go to the place where the food is — the supermarket, most likely. Someone else has done the killing, in the case of animal food, or the primary picking, in the case of vegetables, but essentially the shopper is a gatherer. His or her skills consist in knowing where the good stuff is and tracking it down if it's rare. The shopping experience is given all the trappings of a walk in a magic forest — soft music plays, the colours of packages are supernaturally bright, food is displayed as if it's there by miracle. All you have to do is reach out your hand, as in the Golden Age. And then pay, of course.

Such a system disguises origins. The food in shops is dirt-free, and as bloodless as possible. Yet everything we eat comes — in one way or another — out of the earth.

III

The first garden I can remember was in northern Quebec, where my father ran a small field insect research station. The area was a glacial scrape — a region where the glaciers had removed the topsoil thousands of years ago, scraping down to the granite bedrock. Thousands of years after their retreat, the soil was just a thin layer on top of sand or gravel. My parents used this sandy soil as the basis for their garden. Luckily they had a source of manure, from a lumber camp — in those days, horses were still used in winter, to drag the felled trees down to the lake for eventual transport to the mill by water. My parents ferried boatloads of this manure to their fenced-in sandy patch, where they dug it in. From this unpromising ground they raised — among other things — peas, beans, carrots, radishes, lettuce, spinach, Swiss chard, and even the occasional flower. Nasturtiums are what I remember, and the vivid blossoms of the scarlet runner beans, a favourite with hummingbirds. The moral: almost any patch of dirt can be a garden, with enough elbow grease and horse manure.

That garden occurred in the 1940s, when the war was still going on, horticulture in the form of Victory Gardens was still widely practised, and every morsel of food was treasured.

IV

After the war the post-war boom set in, and attitudes underwent a major change. After a long period of anxiety and hard

SATEC@W.A. PORTER C.I.

The centrepiece of the first United Nations Peace Water Garden, the pond built by students and staff, exhibits diverse aquatic life and is a source of both visual pleasure and scientific interest for the school.

work and tragedy, people wanted more ease in their lives. Military production switched off, the manufacture of consumer goods switched on. Home appliances proliferated: the outdoor clothesline was replaced by the dryer, the wringer washer by the automatic. Supermarkets sprang up. Pre-packaging arrived. Simple-minded abundance was the order of the day.

The period from 1950 to 2000 might be characterized as the Disposable Period. Waste — including pre-planned obsolescence — was no longer seen as an evil and a sin. It became a positive thing, because the more you threw out, the

more you would consume, and that would drive the economy, and everyone would become more prosperous. Wouldn't they?

This model works fine as long as there's an endless supply of goods funnelling into the In end of the pipe. But it breaks down when the source of supply becomes exhausted. The ultimate source of supply is the biosphere itself. But in the fifties, that too appeared to be inexhaustible. And so the party continued. What a thrill, to eat only half of your hamburger, then toss the rest!

There was an undeniable emotional charge to throwing stuff out. Scrimping, saving and hoarding make a person feel poor — think of Scrooge, in *A Christmas Carol* — whereas dispensing largesse, whether in the form of a prize goose, as in Scrooge's case, or in the form of filling up your garbage can with junk you no longer want, makes you feel rich. Saving is heavy, discarding is light. Why do we feel this way? Once we were nomads, and nomads don't carry around grand pianos. They don't hoard food; instead they move to where food is. They leave a light footprint, as the green folk say. Well, it's a theory.

But we can't all be nomads any more. There isn't enough space left for that.

V

Many people gave up their gardens after the war. My parents kept on with theirs, because they said fresh food tasted better. (This is actually true.) The age of full-blown pesticides was just arriving, and that may have had something to do with it as well. My father was an early opponent of widespread pesticide use, partly because this was his field of study. According to him, spraying forests to kill infestations of budworm and sawfly simply arrested the infestation, after which the insects would develop a resistance to the poisons used on them and would continue on their rampage. Meanwhile you'd have killed off their natural enemies, which would no longer be around to fight them. The effects of these poisons on human beings was unknown, but could not be discounted. At that time his views were considered quaint.

Thus the second major garden in my life was in Toronto. Again, the soil was unpromising: heavy clay, which was sticky in the rain but would bake to a hard finish during dry spells. The soil was particularly good for growing giant dandelions and huge clumps of couch grass. It took a lot of work to turn it into anything resembling a garden. Kitchen scraps were composted, fall leaves were dug into the ground by the bushel.

By this time I was a teenager, and was expected to do quite a lot of weeding and watering. News for parents: weeding and watering someone else's garden is not quite as engaging as weeding and watering your own. The high points were the time when I shot a marauding woodchuck with my bow (the arrow was a target arrow, not a hunting arrow, so it bounced off) and the other time when I pulled up all of my father's experimental Jerusalem artichokes by mistake.

Once past my teenage years, I gave up gardening for a time. I'd had enough of it. Also I wasn't in a location that permitted it: I was an itinerent student and sometime teacher and market researcher and writer, and I moved fifteen times in ten years. In the early seventies, however, I found myself on a farm that had a barn with a large supply of well-rotted horse manure, and the temptation was too great to resist. For eight years we grew everything imaginable. To the staples we added corn, kohlrabi, asparagus, currants — red and white — and elderberries. We tried out new methods — potatoes grown in straw, marigolds to catch slugs. We canned, froze, dried; we made sauerkraut, not an experiment I would choose to repeat. We made wine, jams and jellies, beer. We

ISLAND PUBLIC/NATURAL SCIENCE SCHOOL

Students explore the "soundscape" of the naturalized areas around their school as inspiration for art.

raised our own chickens and ducks and sheep; we buried parsnips in holes in the ground, and carrots in boxes of sand in the root cellar.

It was a lot of work. This is one reason people don't do more home gardening.

The other, of course, is lack of land. The number of pumpkins you can raise on your apartment balcony is finite, and your wheat crop in this location would not be large.

VI

Lack of land. Lack of *arable* land. To that we may add "lack of sea," because the sea's resources are being destroyed as fast as the earth's. Soon we may have to add "lack of fresh water" and even "lack of breathable air." There's no free lunch after all.

As a species, we're suffering from our own success. From a population of four million ten thousand years ago, we've increased to six billion today, and growing. The exponential population explosion that has occurred since 1750 was unprecedented in human history, and it will never be repeated. We must slow our growth rate as a species, or face a series of unimaginable environmental and human catastrophes. Arable land is finite, and much of it is rapidly being paved over, eroded, polluted, or depleted. The same rules apply to us as to other animals: no biological population can outlive the exhaustion of its resource base. It's an easy thing to demonstrate to children. Get them an ant farm, feed the ants, watch the ants increase in number. Then cut off the food supply. End of ants.

For homo sapiens, the major question of the twenty-first century will be, *How will we eat?* Already 80 percent of the world's people exist on the starvation borderline. Will we see a sudden enormous crash, as in the mouse-and-lemming cycle? And if so, what then?

These are alarming thoughts to place in the foreword to a kindly and attractive book on school gardening. Such an admirable demonstration of care and careful planning, so much variety, such a symbol of hope. I don't apologize for these thoughts, however: the world I have just described is the one today's children will be facing unless there are some fairly large changes of direction.

The reasons for encouraging the school gardening movement are many. Gardens are educational, teaching as they do many lessons. Food grows in the ground, not in supermarkets; air, soil, sun and water are the four necessary ingredients; composting is a fine notion; front lawns are a water-gobbling waste of space; the individual can be an instrument for positive change; unless you're a geologist, plants are more interesting than gravel; beetles come in many forms; worms are good; nature must be respected; we are part of nature.

All of these are positive concepts, but fifty years ago — even thirty years ago — they would have been viewed as extra, frilly, prissy, goody-goody. Even now, some in our society would place them in this slot: the hard stuff, the right stuff to grind into the minds of children, is how to make a lot of money.

But money's useless when there's nothing to eat. So there's another set of skills to be learned from school gardens: how to grow your own food. Perhaps today's children will need these skills. Perhaps they'll find themselves in some grim collective dedicated to turning golf courses back into market gardens and superhighways into very long grain fields, and front lawns into potato plots. Perhaps the Victory Garden will make a forced comeback due to scarcity.

Or perhaps our species will solve its problems before droughts and famines become endemic.

Then again, perhaps not.

Statistics and historical overviews courtesy of *A Green History of the World,* by Clive Ponting (Penguin) and *Something New Under the Sun: An Environmental History of the Twentieth-Century World,* by J.R. McNeill (Norton)

INTRODUCTION

OVER THE PAST TEN YEARS, school gardening, a once-popular teaching tool in rural and urban communities, has seen a surprising resurgence in urban settings. And as gardeners have grown in knowledge and skill, the school gardening movement itself has become more widely recognized. In 1999, when a survey was conducted across six hundred schools in Toronto, 150 responded with descriptions of their efforts in schoolyard greening. Such extensive involvement in an activity with no formal central organization suggested that the school gardening movement had taken on its own momentum to fill a neglected educational niche. And with good reason. The stories in this book are consistent with stories of schoolyard greening in both the United Kingdom and the United States, all of which report many advantages to children who are given the opportunity to participate in transforming outdoor areas of their school into "learning grounds."

A Breath of Fresh Air celebrates the achievements of gardeners in Toronto's public schools. Parents, students, teachers and grounds staff have created new and beautiful spaces on their school grounds through their dedication, problem-solving skills and organizational abilities. They have understood the benefits — educational, social, psychological and environmental — that diverse green landscapes can bring to school environments, and have engaged with their communities in converting parts of their school grounds into vibrant growing spaces.

This collection of photographs and stories of gardening in some of Toronto's schools offers a window onto these magical outdoor spaces. Projects of different types were selected to provide a representative snapshot of gardening activity across these schools at the end of the millennial year. In each example, teachers and parents offer their insights into what is required for planning these gardens and the opportunities for new learning and hands-on experience they afford.

School gardening depends on support from a number of different sources. The school board's grounds staff have been hailed by many of our school gardeners as some of their most essential allies and advisors. Government agencies, private foundations, non-governmental organizations, banks, businesses and clubs have offered financial support for school gardening projects. In nearly all cases, however, gardening requirements — including plants, tools, soil, soil amendments, structures, materials for pond-building and library resources relating to gardening and school-ground naturalization — have been provided through a combination of community donations and the fundraising efforts of the gardeners themselves.

Toronto's schools' gardens represent one part of a movement to support the growth of ecological literacy. The Toronto District School Board, Canada's largest and first to have a dedicated department of environmental education, has made an important contribution towards focusing formal curriculum in the classroom in a similar direction. To facilitate learning *in, about* and *for* the environment, and to facilitate developing a better understanding of human-environment relationships across subject areas, the Toronto District School Board has introduced three organizing concepts to bring a new ecological dimension to set curriculum:

(1) *Sense of Place* to explore and see our immediate surroundings, both natural and built, and to look beyond the immediate to the larger landscape.

(2) *Ecosystems Thinking* to help us examine how nature works and to understand how natural and human systems are interconnected and interdependent.

(3) *Human Impact* to weigh the consequences, both helpful and harmful, of human interventions into natural systems.

School gardens provide an ideal opportunity to apply these organizing concepts to day-to-day learning. There is no better place than one's own garden plot to learn about a local place and what grows there; about nature at work and the essential services it provides; and about the possible positive or negative effects people's actions have on the natural world.

In addition to illustrating a range of school garden types and examples, we discuss some long-term maintenance implications of the different approaches to schoolyard gardening.

The first chapter of our journey through school gardens explores the many and sometimes surprising benefits gardens offer to teachers and young people alike. In chapter 2, we focus on the excellent opportunities for community-building that school gardening affords. Chapter 3 describes garden types and features using the examples of discrete or self-contained gardens, and in chapter 4, school gardens which are designed as an integral part of school children's play space are described. School grounds as places to share with nature are illustrated in a series of habitat rehabilitation projects in chapter 5, and in chapter 6, Toronto's urban forest and the role schools can play in preserving its shady green canopy are examined. In the last chapter, we explore, through the eyes of experts and educators, some directions that school gardening may take in the future.

A Breath of Fresh Air draws on the experience and collective wisdom of school gardeners in Toronto schools, and is sure to inspire present and future school gardeners anywhere.

A NOTE TO THE READER: In 1998, the Province of Ontario amalgamated the six municipalities of Toronto, York, East York, North York, Scarborough and Etobicoke to create the new City of Toronto. We have retained the former names of schools when referring to them.

I couldn't help but wonder,
if I had the patience, the curiosity,
and a quiet sense of the holy,
what more the field might
still have to reveal ...

— PHYLLIS BRUCE
WILD STONE HEART:
AN APPRENTICE IN THE FIELDS

chapter 1 WHY SCHOOL GARDENS?
A CONVERGENCE OF NATURE'S GIFTS

> There can be no better place than our schools for beginning humanity's greatest task — that of re-connecting ourselves to the natural world.
>
> — ANN COFFEY, "TRANSFORMING SCHOOL GROUNDS," IN *GREENING SCHOOL GROUNDS: CREATING HABITATS FOR LEARNING*

THERE ARE MANY IMPORTANT THINGS to be learned in a garden. The extraordinary burgeoning of gardening as a popular activity — the growth of home gardening, community gardening and the increased naturalization of parks and school properties — speaks of far more than an aesthetic exercise. Gardening is a learning experience involving a rewardingly diverse range of discoveries, knowledge and skills.

In a highly technological society such as ours, gardening reconnects us with the land and feeds our hunger for aspects of human experience missing in our lives. Writer Michael Pollan has aptly described the garden as a place "both real and metaphorical, where nature and culture can be wedded in a way that can benefit both."[1] There is growing awareness that now, more than ever, we need to learn to use nature without damaging it. The lessons a garden can offer about human attitudes and nature's power — as well as its vulnerability to human actions — may prove invaluable to the next generation, who will need to work out their own, more respectful relationship with nature. What better place than school, then, to learn about gardening not only indoors but outdoors as well?

THE INDIVIDUALITY OF GARDENS

Most school gardens are inspired by a wish to see children spend more fulfilling time outside, working co-operatively together, adding beauty, life and colour to their surroundings, learning to care for living things, making a connection with nature and the soil. And within these broader aspirations, each garden takes on a special personality of its own: gardens are as individual as their creators, their spaces and the purposes they are designed to fulfill.

Interviews with teachers and parents who have invested countless volunteer hours in nurturing school garden projects provided us with a remarkable array of approaches to gardening across Toronto schools. Some of our school gardeners had no previous horticultural experience, but they recognized the potential of developing school grounds as new places in which to learn. Their successes depended less on their green thumbs and more on their abilities to draw on community resources and to co-ordinate participation in carrying out their projects. Others, however, were already experienced home gardeners, community gardeners, second- or third-generation gardeners and even professional landscape architects.

SCHOOL GARDENING —
Language for a New Millennium

In *A Breath of Fresh Air,* the word *gardening* is used in a generic sense, to describe *all* planning and planting activities that we have observed in schools. But, as our stories demonstrate, gardening at the beginning of a new millennium embraces many new environmental ideas and ecological concepts that take it beyond the simply practical or aesthetic. School gardening fosters a way of seeing the world from a new vantage point through considerations of healthy ecosystems, water quality, energy use, native and non-native species, natural communities, gardens as habitat and people seeking a new and more co-operative relationship with nature.

Naturalization is a term used to describe the addition of more biologically diverse elements to school grounds. The word was derived from the practice of letting selected slopes, water's edges and lesser-used areas in public parks revert to a more natural state. In its more active form, however, naturalization has come to mean a hands-on approach to converting managed landscapes (typically pavement, grass and trees) into natural spaces through the addition of trees, shrubs and wildflowers, and sometimes by the construction of small ponds.

Naturalized areas require less watering and maintenance and help to soften institutional landscapes.

Habitat rehabilitation involves restoring local flora and stimulating the growth of naturally evolving ecosystems. While displaced ecosystems cannot be recreated in their original forms, this more scientifically based form of restoration effort pays attention to the history of a local area's ecology. The goal of habitat rehabilitation is to let restored areas evolve on their own, relatively free of human intervention, so that, as they mature, they can provide shelter for formerly displaced species.

Greening is often used in a literal sense to describe efforts to increase the green spaces on school property, whether it consists of gardens, areas that have been re-landscaped with trees, shrubs and flowers, or areas which are simply allowed to revert to a more natural state. It may also signal a move towards ecological thinking, which is reflected in changes in the surrounding physical environment. More broadly, the term is used to imply an effort on the part of a group or institution to shift towards more environmentally friendly behaviour and practices.

What these projects have in common, for both experienced and less experienced gardeners, is clarity of purpose. At the outset, participants asked and answered the question, What is this project aiming to accomplish? They knew that purpose determined design. Once a project's purpose was decided, the rest followed: the garden's physical design, the learning opportunities to be built in and the ways in which school community members became involved.

For more than a year, we visited and photographed school gardens. From our findings, we divided these gardens into three types. The first is what some horticulturalists refer to as discrete, or self-contained, gardens, whose wide variety of expressions ranged from aesthetic enhancement, community-building, to food-growing and small habitat creation. The second involves the addition of trees, shrubs and plants to the play area of the school ground; the third focuses on the planting of species and plant communities native to southern Ontario, an approach which fosters the regeneration of natural spaces on school property and eventually provides a limited wild area for scientific and environmental studies. For the purposes of the school garden journey that follows, we have named these three types of gardens *discrete (or self-contained) gardens, landscaping for active play* and *habitat rehabilitation.*

Some school gardening projects harness nature's energies for their caretakers' own use and pleasure, while others are left to their own devices so that nature can regain a foothold in a part of the schoolyard. From these diverse experiences of gardening, students and their teachers can learn both about the uses that humans derive from nature and nature's larger self-sustaining processes.

A HARVEST OF BENEFITS

The immediate and long-term benefits of school-ground improvement to students and school communities have been well documented.[2] These include improved quality of play, greater safety and well-being and enhanced academic achievement. Environmental psychology also offers evidence that greener, more beautiful landscapes favourably affect both students and teachers: stress fades, social interactions increase. Still other benefits for students are the increased ability to think creatively, greater opportunity for hands-on

BENNINGTON HEIGHTS P.S.
Students are taught that insects and arachnids often have a beneficial role in the garden, and should be studied, appreciated and protected.

NORMAN INGRAM P.S.

Observation of growing things in their own garden allows students to develop an appreciation of plant development. They are taught to handle living things gently while exploring their special features.

learning about nature and the creation of a sense of place.

Our garden gives us a feeling of inner peace; the smell of rain and the sound of it can come almost right inside ... it just slows everyone down as they walk down the hall. It's a real sensory boost for us; it adds vitality and lowers everybody's blood pressure here.

— VIVIAN GAULT, TEACHER,
THORNCLIFF PARK PUBLIC SCHOOL

Canadian elementary students spend as much as a quarter of their school day on the grounds outside the school building. Studies show that the management and design of such spaces convey messages to children that influence their attitudes and behaviour.[3] Traditional paved fenced schoolyards, while practical for surveillance and some kinds of outdoor activities, offer little opportunity for genuine creative play. Compared with the rich and stimulating indoor environment of the contemporary classroom, the conventional, austere, grass-and-asphalt schoolyard limits experiential learning. Redesigning school grounds to provide more diverse landscapes, surfaces and activities helps to harmonize the school's overall environment with the goals of classroom learning.[4]

Many researchers, educators and parents recognize the potential greener schoolyard spaces have to provide new educational, recreational and social experiences for children. Those who have begun to transform their school grounds report that outdoor stimulation enhances the satisfaction and pleasure of classroom learning.

PLAYING AND LEARNING IN SCHOOL GARDEN AREAS

More than a decade of school gardening has provided ample opportunity to observe and analyze the improved quality of

Nature's artistry demonstrated in the money plant, also known as silver dollar or "honesty."

well-being, play, teaching and learning that naturalized areas give their school communities. One of the clearest demonstrations of the worth of such transformed spaces is the behaviour of the children themselves: one researcher noted that when 10 percent of a schoolyard was naturalized to include areas of refuge, activity in those areas occupied nearly half of the students' outdoor playtime.[5] A teacher from a school with a community watershed restoration project on adjoining parkland reported that "the children might not be having a successful day, but when we go into the garden and get the time to explore physically, there is a calming effect; it becomes a different environment and place." Another teacher from the same school described the naturalized area's particular magic as important "for my sixty second vacations — taking a moment to look out the window and catch my breath!"

Natural elements in play areas increase young children's interest in their spaces and add new stimulus to their imaginative play. The addition of shrubs, trees or planted beds makes play spaces safer by slowing down their movements, and changing hard surfaces to softer ones such as wood chips or sand creates places for children to tumble or fall with less chance of injury. According to the study *Nature Nurtures*, commissioned by Evergreen, one of Canada's foremost organizations that bring nature to schools, greened school grounds are particularly beneficial to children in middle childhood:

This is the time in a child's development when the full diversity of life and form in

LEASIDE C.I.

A student prepares the soil for the planting of a weed-resistant native wildflower garden.

nature registers, forms patterns, sets priorities and establishes the building blocks of adult sensibilities about self, others and the world at large ... If there is one time in a child's life when interacting with nature in a schoolyard is crucial, it is in middle childhood. But the outdoor learning of middle childhood is not just about nature. This learning is linked to establishing ethical principles, learning to get along with others, understanding delayed gratification and building the language and social skills to negotiate a place in the world.[6]

A final compelling argument for increasing children's opportunities to learn outdoors is the clear evidence that such learning has a significant effect on academic achievement. A 1998 study *(Closing the Achievement Gap: Using the Environment as an Integrating Context for Learning)* of forty American schools with programs focusing on learning in outdoor environments showed that the students in these programs scored consistently higher on achievement tests. The study also reconfirmed the effectiveness of this kind of hands-on learning in developing problem-solving skills, a more comprehensive understanding of the world and an appreciation of the diversity of viewpoints within a democratic society. Finally, student attitudes, behaviour, and attendance, as well as teacher morale, improved in all cases

When you're putting plants in the ground, there's a bond between the plants and the kids; it's just magic.

— HEIDI CAMPBELL

TDSB/EVERGREEN SCHOOLGROUND GREENING DESIGN FACILITATOR

TWENTIETH STREET P.S.

An island of life and colour brightens the path to the school door.

recorded. While this study was not focused on learning *about* the natural environment, its results clearly illustrate that learning *in* the outdoor environment gives students a clearer understanding of theoretical concepts as they observe them in action.[7]

Many of those involved in school-ground naturalization especially value a longer-term advantage for students: a heightened awareness and understanding of the needs of healthy ecosystems to support human life and well-being. Given the pace at which the growing world population is consuming global resources and depleting the earth's "ecological services" (air, water, the ozone layer, forests), there is an urgent need to examine the effects of human activity on both living and non-living systems. Adding an ecological outlook to learning in a garden allows students to see new connections between their own experiences and the world outside the school.

chapter 2

COMMUNITIES GROWING TOGETHER

INVOLVING THE COMMUNITY IN SCHOOL GARDENING

As we move towards the twenty-first century, the great challenge of our time is to create ecologically sustainable communities, communities in which we can satisfy our needs and aspirations without diminishing the chances of future generations. We need to become ecologically literate, and the best place to acquire ecological literacy is the school garden.

— FRITJOF CAPRA, *TURN, TURN, TURN: UNDERSTANDING NATURE'S CYCLES*

THE DESIGN, PREPARATION, PLANTING and maintenance of a school garden offers many opportunities for community-building. Transforming a portion of a schoolyard from a grass, dirt or asphalt space into a living and blooming landscape is a complex project, one that involves a broad range of skills and as many willing participants.

A garden community can be as small as a teacher and a class with a short-term plan, or it can be as large as a joint parent–teacher garden committee with a long-term plan that involves the entire school's participation and requires truckloads of new soil, large-sized trees and a variety of themed garden plots. From its very inception, a school garden project has the potential to grow into a community of planners, advisers, supporters, contributors, funders, caretakers,

plant experts and designers, not to mention the hard workers who prepare the soil and set the chosen plants into the earth.

Reaching out to discover community resources is a valuable first step in getting started. Some would-be gardeners begin by visiting other school gardeners and their gardens. Others gather ideas by visiting parks, nurseries, conservation authorities, outdoor education centers, arboretums or local natural spots such as ravines. Such preliminary visits often blossom into ongoing cordial relationships and exchanges between schools and local plant experts. Once the idea of a garden is set into motion, schools might discover that there are experienced gardeners or even landscape architects right in their midst, among their own staff and parents. The following stories offer a glimpse into the possible kinds of community-building that school gardening can engender.

OSSINGTON/OLD ORCHARD PUBLIC SCHOOL

Trailblazers in Greening a Downtown School

In the mid-1980s, a group of parents approached school principal Ted Curry with an ambitious vision: concerned about the lack of green space available at their children's

school, they proposed a transformation of the vast, feature-less expanse of pavement that stretched between Ossington and Old Orchard Public Schools. Curry, whose background included experience in outdoor education as principal of the Island Public School, joined in the parents' early exploratory conversations on school-ground greening, and assisted in taking their inquiries to the area superintendent and, eventually, to the Board. The Board granted its approval to the proposed relandscaping project on condition that the school community itself raise all the funds. The Board also obtained the assistance of the Learnxs Foundation to sponsor the project. The parents, two of whom were landscape architects, formed a gardening committee and set to work. Despite the scope of the project, they were confident that a concerted effort would raise the necessary funds and attract the volunteer labour required to turn nearly a square block of asphalt into a green space for the school community.

"Once they got the okay, they just ran with it; their enthusiasm was infectious," recalled Curry. "They had all the ideas, sought a phenomenal number of grants, made plans, got contacts and donations, and did it in phases. It took two to three years." With the asphalt surface removed, the ambitious and complex plan slowly became a reality. The central portion of the former pavement was made into a grassy playing field. The slopes of the school's ravine setting, once the banks of Toronto's now-buried Garrison Creek, were partly naturalized with native plants and partly terraced to provide a series of garden plots for the students. An orchard was planted to honour the site's farming-community roots, trees were added to provide shade and variety, and the students wove twig baskets around the trunks to protect the trees through their early years. An "aviary" of shrubs was planted along one edge to provide food, shelter and habitat for birds and butterflies. As one of the first major gardening projects in Toronto, Ossington's success has inspired many other schools.

OSSINGTON/OLD ORCHARD P.S.
Pioneers in school-ground naturalization, OOOPS gardeners recaptured the feeling of a ravine setting and a farming heritage.

A key component of the Ossington parents' vision was to make the garden an integral part of the school community. "They involved the staff, so that every classroom would have a plot," Curry noted. "Nearly all the staff came on board, and they went out and planted their choice of crops. The teachers did a good bit of gardening at the beginning, and we had parents who would come to help them." For nearly five years, Ossington was fortunate enough to have its own resident gardening instructor. Horticulturalist Dagmar Baur was brought on staff to make gardening an integral part of the curriculum. In tune with the seasons, she took small groups of students outside for planting and garden maintenance during the warm weather, and inside for gardening, science and seed-planting projects during the cold winter months.

Participation in gardening efforts waxed and waned over the years, but Ossington's large-scale garden remains its trademark, and the spirit of volunteerism is still strong. "We have many parents who come to this school because of the garden," said Lynn Murray, a teacher who has been an active gardener for all of her thirteen years at the school. "I don't think Ossington/Old Orchard would be nearly as popular without the garden."

The Garden Committee has its own fund, holds an annual bake sale, popcorn days and a "vine sale" in the school corridor, where paper vine leaves can be purchased for a dollar each by garden supporters. At regular school-funding events, the committee sells garden mugs and T-shirts that feature its logo of nesting birds. Murray was very optimistic about the resurgence in participation. "We now have a group of parents from the kindergarten, a new wave like the old wave ten years ago. They're all young and enthusiastic, and they even have a band and play instruments. They played during our whole Harvest Festival!" (The Harvest Festival is one of two annual school events that bring the whole gardening community together to clean up the grounds.)

The effect of the garden on the students is palpable. "Gardens make people nicer," Murray observed. "They also give them a sense of belonging. Kids love to hide and have secret little places, and we've got lots of them. And children have to feel that oneness with nature, especially when you're in the city, where everything is so controlled. In the spring when we're planting, we talk about being sensitive to the plants and the bugs. We don't kill anything — everything's important."

Despite having to fundraise for the special maintenance needs that the terraced slopes now require, Murray expressed optimism for the future of Ossington's garden. "The new young teachers are very environmentally conscious, although right now they're overwhelmed by the job. But once they are more established in their teaching, I have no doubt that the garden will continue. Plus, new parents are always coming up, and it only really takes a few parents who are gung-ho to organize, and then everyone follows and comes along."

OSSINGTON/OLD ORCHARD P.S.
This ladybird beetle rests on a comfrey plant, awaiting discovery by exploring young gardeners.

FLEMING PUBLIC SCHOOL
Strengthening Links with Neighbours and Nature

Some gardening efforts start more simply. Grade 5 teacher Irene Hodges and Grade 8 teacher Judy Thorne at Fleming Public School felt strongly that involving parents in an effort to beautify their "plain" school would reinforce a feeling of ownership in the school. They invited parents, some with little English, to join their children in planting fifteen hundred tulip bulbs purchased with the proceeds of a student penny drive. Despite a downpour of rain on the Saturday appointed for the planting, eager students, teachers and a large number of parents worked together cheerfully to get all the bulbs into the ground. "The next spring when beautiful tulips started opening up and you saw this glorious amount of colour ... we were just so proud of ourselves. We could do anything now!" enthused Hodges. Exchanges, sometimes translated from or into English by children, flew back and forth between neighbours and teachers, with inquiries and answers about where bulbs might be found and the best way to plant them in home gardens. Gardening in the front of the school had become a form of conversation with the surrounding community, which would lead, the following year, to a more ambitious kind of gardening project behind the school.

This time the project involved neighbours who were members of a local conservation group called Friends of the Rouge Watershed (FRW), whose mandate is to engage community participation in the restoration of Rouge Park, Canada's second largest urban park. FRW has been working for more than ten years as part of a large partnership called the Rouge Park Alliance to restore ecological integrity to the degraded river valley and, in the words of the park's management plan, make it "a sanctuary for nature and the human spirit." Some of FRW's board members are teachers, and the educational benefits of watershed restoration had not

FLEMING P.S.

The wildflower and butterfly garden offers a colourful view for neighbours and a world of natural wonders for children to care for, study and enjoy.

escaped them. They got in touch with Irene Hodges and Judy Thorne. "We're always involved in proactive, community-based conservation," remarked Jim Robb, general manager of FRW. "So the idea of education going hand in hand with conservation was something we felt really strongly about, particularly in the long-term perspective."

Over the years, Robb has played a key role in involving up to two thousand school children a year in doing plantings throughout the Rouge River Valley, and teaching them about local ecology. Focused as they are on community-based nature conservation efforts, FRW members feel strongly that children, and particularly urban children who live in areas near nature restoration projects, can benefit enormously from hands-on participation in the rehabilitation of local sites. "It's so important because they don't get the same exposure any of us had when we were younger and there were more open spaces nearby," stated Robb. "And they're going to be going into the valley, they're going to be the custodians of the valley in the future, so we wanted to try to get at an early age a kind of a love for nature within them."

The Morningside tributary of the Rouge River runs through the valley immediately adjacent to the school property in Scarborough. Under FRW supervision, Fleming's elementary school children, teachers and assisting high-school co-op students participated in three separate plantings with restoration ecologists to bring new life to this area. But going off school property, even to an immediately adjoining area, required permission forms and organizational work for classroom teachers, so FRW and the Fleming staff had another idea. They decided to develop a wildflower and butterfly garden "on this side of the fence," right on school property, which would allow ease of access for ongoing maintenance and use and, at the same time, would reflect the wild beauty and the native species of their local river valley. (How they developed this natural space is described in detail in chapter 3.)

Last year in June, Mrs. Pink and I combined our classes for a picnic near the butterfly garden. The children brought their lunches and some snacks to share. While one teacher did a group activity with the children, the other took small groups, three or four, into the butterfly garden, to find animals and plants and to compare how they are the same and different. They found seeds, bugs, birds, flowers, leaves, eggs on the underside of leaves, and other interesting natural objects and creatures. We followed up in the classroom with discussions, drawings and labelling.

AMANDA GREEN, TEACHER, FLEMING PUBLIC SCHOOL

At Fleming Public School, gardening has strengthened links with neighbours and built a strong formal partnership with a local nature restoration group. "Tulips in the front and nature in the back" has proved to be a very successful strategy for engaging parents, students and ecologists in the beauty and the science of school gardening.

THORNCLIFF PARK PUBLIC SCHOOL

Bonding with Seniors and the Soil

Canada's largest elementary school (K–5) is located in east-central Toronto, the former East York, situated in a community of towering apartment buildings. Thorncliff Park Public School has twenty kindergartens and an enrolment of nearly fourteen hundred students to serve its high-density neighbourhood. But one feature of this school that makes it an oasis in the midst of such highly urbanized life is its interior space, lovingly landscaped in three courtyard gardens.

Vivian Gault, a Grade 2 teacher and head of the Thorncliff Park Garden Committee, has used her own family gardening tradition and her love of soil to instill in her students an eagerness for learning about all growing things. She teaches her students how to be involved in creating beautiful spaces within their school.

Although they had been tended on and off for twelve to fourteen years, Thorncliff's courtyard gardens had fallen into a sad state. Gault's eighty-year-old father offered to come in once or twice a week to help with weeding and maintenance, and to get the children involved in planting. "I had a grade two class of apartment-dwelling children who have little opportunity to get out and get dirty in soil. It seemed natural to want to become involved," she stated simply. "You get the teachers like me who love working with the kids and the soil and worms and things like that," she laughed, "although there weren't enough of us. It wasn't a formal 'Let's get together and plant.' It was almost like staff saying, 'I've got some of this at home,

THORNCLIFF PARK P.S.
Courtyard gardens provide sheltered spaces for planting and attracting birds; students help keep feeders full.

why don't I bring it in?' 'Why doesn't my class go out and we'll plant some hostas around that back tree?' 'I'd really like to learn about vegetables, so why don't we have the grade ones plant carrots and onions and potatoes?'"

Vivian Gault's father and a friend began to come regularly to Thorncliff Park to work with the students in the courtyards. Gault felt that the bond forged between the seniors and the children became one of the most precious aspects of their mutual gardening experience. "They've learned the wonderful lesson that's so dear to my

THORNCLIFF
PARK P.S.

*In three treasured
courtyard gardens,
children in Canada's
largest elementary
school plant and
watch the process
of regeneration
and growth.*

who are recent immigrants to Canada, often have their first encounters with soil in the Thorncliff Park gardens. Some have never seen a root before. Gault described their reaction:

> "You can tell when a girl with a long *shalwar kameez* (which is the clothing of many of the children of our school) and a *hijab* around her head never had a chance to put a trowel in her hand before, or a rake, or to put her feet on a hoe or a pitchfork trying to get the soil turned over. Her look of absolute sheer pleasure shows that this is the first time she's ever done it."

For all students, Gault says, the experience of growing and eating what they grow is an invaluable experience. "One year my class planted some vegetables, carrots, tomatoes and onions. We made soup with some of the produce, not a great volume … but token things so that the children would know where our food comes from. It's an introduction for kids to all aspects of the soil and what grows in it, and what you have to do to make things grow in it."

The three courtyards of Thorncliff Park offer special places of beauty and solace to many in the busy school community. "We have many children in our school with special needs, and the gardens are a perfect place to take them. We have autistic children. We have dyslexic children. We have hearing-impaired children. And you can see these children with their educational assistants going out, just getting a breath, looking at beauty, learning and finding, literally, a breath of fresh air."

CHURCHILL PUBLIC SCHOOL
Adopting a Garden

Yet another form of community building can come from school garden adoption. Chris Kaye has been Scout Leader to the 18th Toronto Scouts for eight years, and for six of those years her troop has met at Churchill Public School in the

heart, the connection with these two seniors. In fact, some of my former students, now in or finished with high school, come back and know my dad by name. Five or six or seven years down the road they remember him: 'Oh, remember when you did this with my class, wasn't that fun!'"

Children who have grown up in high-rise apartments, or

CHURCHILL P.S.

"What kind of leaf is it?" becomes an interesting question as plant diversity increases in Churchill's native plant garden.

former North York. She sought a way to show her gratitude for this use of the school. "Nobody ever asked anything of us," she remarked. "So we thought, 'We have to give something back.'" The "something" they suggested to the principal of Churchill was community service in the school's rather overgrown ornamental garden. Parents had planned this traditional flower garden in the 1980s, and laid out a few trees, shrubs and a seating area for students in a corner of the playground.

The garden represented a first phase of a more ambitious but never-completed project. The parents had moved on, and the garden had been left to grow more or less on its own. The Churchill garden had been an example of a decorative school garden, but without committed gardeners over the long term, it had lost its high-maintenance design. Ornamental gardens often become overgrown by weeds if they lack constant care and attention. Other than the valiant attentions of a parent who had single-handedly undertaken to do some maintenance, little had been done in the Churchill garden for nearly three years. Kaye felt the site was a perfect place where her Scouts could work towards a number of environmental badges. She recognized the potential of using the garden as a place to teach children about native plants, habitat and herbs, an exercise that could also transform the garden into a more self-sustaining, native perennial garden. The principal was delighted with the proposal of a gardening partnership, and the Scouts set out to fundraise for some new plants.

Since the adoption of the garden by the 18th Scouts and Chris Kaye, all the teachers and students at Churchill have agreed to take on the garden as a community project. "Especially the younger grades," reported the energetic Kaye. "They are very, very enthusiastic." Churchill classes have adopted gardening on a rotation plan, with every class committed to a full week of care, except for junior kindergarten classes who do a day instead of a full week. Each week

CHURCHILL P.S.

Restored by local Scouts, the naturalized garden has blossomed. Here one class learns about the garden as a home for birds.

the students walk through the garden to pick up litter and refill the bird-feeders, which encourages them to take responsibility for the garden.

"I don't think there's one Scout who doesn't have the gardening badge now," Kaye reported of her own troop, "and the environment badge." But her Scouts are growing up. She dreams of persuading the middle school next door to start a garden. "In grades seven, eight and nine, I think they should have a garden to work on, too." She's working with some of her Scouts who have moved up to the middle school, teaching them to write a proposal to the school to ask permission to garden there. For Chris Kaye's Scouts and the Churchill students, gardening is far more than a landscape: it's the centre of a growing, skills-building community.

RUNNYMEDE PUBLIC SCHOOL
Getting Everyone Involved

Help and ideas for school gardens can come from many different quarters. When the Environment Committee at west-central Toronto's Runnymede Public School began its

CHURCHILL P.S.

work in the early 1990s, it drew its inspiration for a naturalized garden from an article about a Kew Beach School garden at the other end of the city. Parent Karen Yukich made a simple first move in this direction by encouraging the existing school Playground Committee to plant some additional trees and think a bit more about native trees. She then teamed up with student-teacher Karyn Morris who agreed to have her Grades 4 and 5 students design a naturalized garden, with fundraising and organizing help from the parent–teacher Garden Committee. The spot chosen for the garden was the steep grassy slope that ran behind and beside the school.

RUNNYMEDE P.S.

The diversity of form, colour and texture found in the garden provide inspiration for art projects.

Since planting a naturalized garden in the early 1990s was still quite a novel thing to do in an urban environment, Runnymede held a public meeting for the local community and explained its intention of developing a garden that would have a somewhat different aesthetic from traditional flower gardens. As the school's Nature Study Garden took shape, teacher Ann Lakoff discovered a willing advisor in High Park staff gardener Terry Fahey. The school decided to choose for its garden the theme of "expanding the borders of High Park," seeking to reflect in its naturalized area the native vegetation found within its local park. Fahey visited

the school and presented a slide show of park plants. He also brought plant samples from the park greenhouse for the school, along with advice as to which plants were more suited to sun, shade and various soil conditions.

In 1998, there was a surge of renewed interest in the schoolyard, and a group of parents came forward to form a Yard Committee, which included a garden subgroup. "I joined that committee as a teacher, and got another teacher on it as well to create that linkage. This parents' committee has been very strong for about two, two and a half years now," stated Lakoff. "We've been doing October clean-up

RUNNYMEDE P.S.

days, a lot of clipping and trimming. And then in the spring we've been doing a planting day. So a day in October, a day in May, and these have been really well-attended by the student body and the community and parents. Just a really nice sort of atmosphere, getting people out to the garden." (More details on the development of this project can be found in chapter 5.)

For school gardeners, gardening can be more about building community than about becoming plant experts. "It's about connecting with other people, connecting with resources. Don't try to reinvent the wheel," observed Yukich. "Visit other sites, interview the people who worked on them, or community groups such as a horticultural society. There are so many places you can connect with."

ISLANDS OF LIFE
chapter 3

DISCRETE GARDENS

We think that we're planting things, but we're really planting seeds of conservation, understanding and ethics.

— JIM ROBB, FRIENDS OF THE ROUGE WATERSHED

THE MAJORITY OF GARDENS we observed in Toronto schools are *discrete* (or *self-contained) gardens.* These are well-defined, bounded plots maintained for a number of specific purposes. They may be *aesthetic* (made up of single species, mixed annuals, perennials, native and exotic species chosen for their decorative qualities); *themed* (a pizza garden, for example); *heritage* (dedicated to growing traditional seeds to protect local genetic diversity); or *mixed* (a combination of any of the above). There is interest, too, in *native plant community* gardens, which familiarize students with local species and which share habitat requirements, and in s*mall habitat* gardens such as butterfly gardens and ponds, which feature plant species that provide food and shelter for small animals and insects during the different stages of their lives.

Two features distinguish a discrete garden — its planners or planters select and arrange its contents (whether annual or perennial), and it requires ongoing maintenance to keep it well cultivated. Discrete gardens are the most labour-intensive type of garden as they require soil amendments (that is, the addition of organic materials such a compost or leaf mulch to improve the quality of the soil) and regular weeding and watering. Even when they are composed of native species or designed to attract small wildlife such as butterflies or birds, these gardens — unlike the habitat

rehabilitation projects described in chapter 5 — are not intended to go wild. As a result, discrete gardens offer the most potential for participation in their design and long-term maintenance.

We have separated the discrete gardens we visited into four types: (1) border and ornamental gardens; (2) native plant and small habitat gardens; (3) food and herb gardens; and (4) pond and bog gardens. These gardens provide excellent educational opportunities because they all need ongoing hands-on involvement. Teachers and students who plan and care for these discrete gardens are exposed to a range of practical learning opportunities, such as measurement and mapping; soil composition and amendment; plant identification, selection and propagation; planting methods; weeding and pruning; watering and wise water use; and cleanup. They learn first-hand about their local soil and how to make suitable plant selections for different kinds of soil conditions, and how to consider the light, space and moisture requirements of their preferred mix of plants. Once the planting is completed, they experience the joys of watching their planning and work yield the magic of growing things, transforming a piece of their landscape into an "island of life."

They also discover that gardening is not without its challenges and how important it is to find out what does *not* work! As urban dwellers, many of us have lost contact with the soil, and we may be surprised to discover that nature in its complexity can hold surprises, even in a small gardening plot. Learning from mistakes is one of the teaching

experiences that gardens can offer new gardeners. "Each thing we try is an experiment," teacher Kathy Caulfield of Broadacres Public School offers as a suggestion to others. "If it doesn't work, it doesn't work. We try ideas the kids would like to try even if we don't think they'll work, because that's how we learn." And when there's a problem, extensive garden expertise is available within the community and the problem becomes an opportunity for making new contacts.

Planning, of course, is a key component of all successful gardening. For those who wish to plant discrete gardens, an essential up-front planning consideration is maintenance during the summer, the heart of the gardening season. Provision must be made for weeding and watering through the months when schools are not in session.

For beginners a discrete garden is a practical place to start, if we bear in mind the advice to "start small" offered by many successful school gardeners. A discrete garden is a manageable space to measure, plan, plant, nurture and maintain. Yet gardening on this small scale in no way limits the degree of creativity that can go into the garden's design. An impressive assortment of discrete garden types is found in Toronto schools. In the border and ornamental group, we found gardens with tulip borders and sunflower patches; an ABC garden with a plant species for each letter of the alphabet; wildflower and ethnic gardens; a peace garden; a "kindergarden"; a rustic garden; and a courtyard shade garden. In the native plant and small habitat group, school projects include butterfly gardens; a bird sanctuary; a "life zone" garden to teach plant identification; and "living walls" that provide both habitat and natural outdoor space dividers.

Despite the challenges of summer, there are schools involved in food and herb gardens. Among them are vegetable gardens; beds of fragrant herbs; pizza gardens; a permaculture garden (incorporating some ecological principles based on "permanent agriculture" methods); a "three sisters" garden demonstrating traditional native plantings of corn, beans and squash; an Aboriginal herb garden; and a heritage seed garden.

The last group of discrete gardens features ponds and bogs as aquatic gardening projects. Of particular interest among these were a pond with a solar water pump, a water-filtering pond, and a pond that became a contested home for ducks.

BORDER AND ORNAMENTAL GARDENS

There are few things so able to add colour and visual variety to a landscape as ornamental gardens. From windowsills and window boxes to formal gardens, people of all means have sought to beautify their outdoor living spaces with the showy blooms and decorative foliage of ornamental plants. In cooler, northern climates, there has long been an interest in importing non-native ornamental plants for their larger blossoms, brighter colours and varied forms. For all their aesthetic advantages, however, non-native species prompt

SATEC@W. A. PORTER C.I.

An ornamental garden brightens the front of this school.

several environmental considerations that might influence the extent of their inclusion in school gardens. They require great care in transporting and cultivating them, their maintenance is labour intensive and they often require regular watering. Most non-native ornamental plants are beneficial or benign, yet a few of these species (purple loosestrife, for example) have proved to be invasive when they have escaped from gardens into neighbouring natural environments. There, finding no natural predators or controls, they have overwhelmed native species and, in some cases, radically altered ecosystems. When planting a school garden and making selections, therefore, it is important to learn how to protect local species and ecosystems.

Perhaps the simplest types of discrete gardens are the border and ornamental garden. In a linear school landscape, rows of single- or mixed-species plantings can add life and colour to the front of a building, the edge of a fence or an entrance path. Planting this type of traditional garden can be an excellent starting point in gaining gardening experience for larger projects.

NORMAN INGRAM P.S.

Word-scavenging for building science vocabulary finds a new setting in the outdoor classroom.

NORMAN INGRAM PUBLIC SCHOOL

A Mixed Ornamental Garden

An excellent example of a mixed ornamental garden is the colourful and hospitably shaded space that graces the front of Norman Ingram Public School, located in the eastern reaches of North York. This project also provides an example of a successful transition in school garden management. The garden was conceived by former principal and avid gardener Betty Lamont as a natural habitat where children could play and study plants, insects and birds, and which would involve people from the community. The scale of the planting required to create the garden was ambitious. In true community spirit, teachers, parents and interested neighbours, along with Lamont, donated plants. A grant from the Friends of

HUMBER VALLEY VILLAGE P.S.
The garden's floral mural was a gift from Etobicoke School of the Arts students.

Blackwell, saddened at the thought of losing a very special school resource, decided to take the plunge as novice gardeners. A brief attempt at handling the maintenance on their own, however, made them realize that they needed help. They put out a rallying call to the community and organized a series of weeding and planting sessions. Parents, students and neighbours arrived, eager and willing to work. From these "Weed and Feed" sessions, a fresh spirit of participation emerged, as well as a renewed effort from the school's Environment Club, donations of plants and shrubs and an offer of assistance from parent Linda Schwartz, who was to become the guiding light of the restored garden.

The garden at Norman Ingram has become a hub of co-operation. A group of Grade 6 students teamed up with Don Mills Collegiate students and built benches. The Environment Club has done regular weeding and has enjoyed observing the many plants, birds and insects sheltering in the garden. The school added a set of composters to the garden and established a food-waste collection program that offers students the first-hand experience of watching scraps turn into rich compost. Teacher-librarian Kathy Kay enumerated some of the activities that lure teachers and classes outside. "They do word-scavenging, scavenger hunts for vocabulary-building, as well as science-scavenging," she began. "And I work with ESL students and special education students. I take all my kids out, and some work on English colour words and texture words, or just the simple basic vocabulary. Others work on more advanced vocabulary and creative writing, in terms of things that are happening in the garden." Joshi teaches multi-handicapped children, and says the garden is a special place for them. "I think it brings out a whole different side of children. You see children differently when they're outside," she reflects, "showing enthusiasm about things that in the classroom you might not see."

the Environment Fund of Canada Trust enabled the school to complete the landscaping and fulfill its objectives of providing colour and beauty, attracting birds and butterflies, providing taste and fragrance (through the inclusion of herbs), and attracting the neighbours to this new oasis. The garden grew and thrived under Lamont's care.

Unfortunately, only a year and a half after starting the gardening project, Lamont retired. Without a formal arrangement for their ongoing maintenance, the lovingly planted beds gradually lapsed into neglect. And, as the garden lost its manicured appearance, there was talk of grassing the area over. Two teachers, Maggie Joshi and Janis

NORMAN INGRAM P.S.

Students enjoy shade, colour, fragrance and a peaceful place to learn. The garden is also a special place for teaching the school's multi-handicapped children.

HUMBER VALLEY VILLAGE PUBLIC SCHOOL
A Friendship Garden

Students and visitors to Humber Valley Village Junior and Middle School, located in Etobicoke, are greeted by an extraordinary flourish of colour as they approach the school. A bright floral mural on the school's wall forms a backdrop to the Friendship Garden, a co-operative project involving the entire school community. An initiative of the Parent Council, the Friendship Garden was designed from its inception to engage the participation of all the school's teachers and classrooms. Parents Lily Tucker and Grace Andrews, the latter a master gardener, secured funding and involved the students in the garden's planning and design. Science teacher Janet Bartolini, who is also the co-ordinator of the Garden Club, described the day when the garden plan was ready to be laid out: "The design was on a map. We took the students out to do the scale measuring, actually transferring the plan from the map to the ground. It was a great exercise in scale mapping; the kids actually plotted out where the gardens would be."

The Friendship Garden is divided into nineteen plots, which allow ease of access and distribution of responsibility for the garden's care. This collection of discrete gardens has made it possible to landscape some beds with shrubs and perennials and to invite classrooms to plant other beds according to themes of their choice. One class planted a pizza garden. Another, when doing a curriculum unit on Japan, chose to plant a Japanese garden. Still another, as a memory aide for learning about native plants, designed an ABC garden, which included an example of a native plant beginning with each letter of the alphabet. The result is an arresting and colourful garden containing a mix of ornamental plants, edible plants and native Ontario species. The stunning floral mural at the entrance was a gift from the students of the Etobicoke School for the Arts, which adds a special atmosphere to this outdoor space.

In covering the Grade 6 unit on the diversity of living things, one of the teachers used the garden regularly to take students out to observe growing things. Every year, Lenore Alexander and her Grade 3 class plant a "three sisters" garden, with the traditional corn, bean and squash crops that provided food staples for Aboriginal peoples in Ontario. Alexander then uses the garden as the basis for teaching Science, Social Studies and reading comprehension.

Individual classes water and weed their own plots. The Garden Club, with students from Grades 1 to 5, works in the garden on Mondays at lunchtime under the guidance of Bartolini. On Friday, she runs a club called Weed Whackers for middle-school students who help with the heavier garden work. "Weeding is the huge issue," Bartolini stated frankly. "The kids are willing to do that for only so long, and then they lose interest. So we've ended up having the Parent Council organize two weeding mornings, one in October and one in May."

LEASIDE C.I.
Spring planting for a weed-resistant native wildflower garden.

NATIVE PLANTS AND SMALL HABITAT GARDENS

In North America, gardens were once small enclaves of cultivated space where gardeners struggled against the forces of nature and the wild spaces that threatened to reclaim their hard-won clearings. Today, on the contrary, it is the wilderness that is rapidly shrinking and becoming fragmented. Worldwide, ever-increasing human-dominated space and relentless human activity are threatening the earth's natural areas and the creatures that call them home. As the wilderness shrinks, the biological diversity of the planet is becoming impoverished.

A new movement in gardening is striving to counter this trend, however. Increasing numbers of pioneer natural landscapers are working to support local biodiversity through the creation of gardens that are ecological sanctuaries. The ideal for these gardeners is not merely to gather and plant individual native species, but to mimic nature through recreating native plant communities, or parts of them. In this way, even in small backyards and schoolyards, gardening can reflect and enhance the area's native vegetation.

LEASIDE COLLEGIATE INSTITUTE
A Method to Reduce Weeding

The movement to repopulate barren spaces with native vegetation has inspired research into ways of reducing the major burden of school gardeners' summer difficulties: weeding and watering. Arthur Beauregard, the manager of Natural Environments and Horticulture for the Parks and Recreation Department of the City of Toronto, generously volunteered

LEASIDE C.I.
A lush array of native wildflowers greets returning students in September.

his time and expertise to participate in a school demonstration project that would help increase the success rate of native species plantings. "Weeds are the main problem around naturalization," Beauregard stated. "The second problem is generally irrigation and trimming."

In partnership with a group of students and staff members from Youth Challenge International, Beauregard worked on a naturalization project at Leaside Collegiate Institute in East York. "We undertook this operation to demonstrate technically, more than anything else, how these projects could work, because we had had some pretty good success with limiting the weeds. But what we discovered was that the

technical barriers aren't the major ones. It's just getting the work organized and properly maintained — that is the main problem."

One of the first obstacles to weed-free gardening that Beauregard cited was a simple lack of patience on the part of would-be gardeners. "People aren't patient. We live in North America where people want the instant effect." He advises against simply removing a section of turf to start a garden. "The most important thing to do before we start moving grass or decide to put in a native bed is to determine the inventory of weed seeds and perennial weeds in the area. You can't really do it in the early spring because you won't see anything: they haven't started to grow yet."

The best way to prepare a future garden site, in Beau-regard's expert opinion, is to strip off the grass and observe the empty site for one season. This process is called *fallowing,* or letting the land lie dormant. "There can be a whole education in just seeing what's growing, noticing for example if it's an annual weed or a perennial weed growing from seed. Then you could have the opportunity to find out how plants grow. The first season should be taken up with actually cutting the annual weeds down, or pulling them up before they go to seed, and in digging out the complete root system of the perennial weeds. And if you have an infestation of field bindweed (a type of wild morning glory) in your lawn, for example, *never put a bed there!* Because field bindweed will ruin it forever; it's a horror story!"

In the second year, Beauregard suggests setting plants into a two-to-three-centimeter layer of sand mulch. "Now the sand will do a number of things, but mostly why you have it there is to suppress the germination of any weed seeds that still happen to be on the surface. The other advantage to sand is, if you're growing native plants, a two-centimetre layer of sand will markedly cut down — by a factor of about 95 percent — the number of weed seeds. The only thing you have to be careful of, when you know you haven't depleted

the weed seed store, and you're using the sand mulch, is that you can't go in and start cultivating. Because, as soon as you do that, you're bringing the seeds to the surface. So you just have to leave it alone."

Beauregard and his colleagues from Youth Challenge International engaged the high school students in designing the native plant bed. "We provided them with lists of plants and descriptions of plants and their heights, and, with coaching from Parks and Recreation staff, they actually designed it."

The garden at Leaside bloomed spectacularly over its first summer. But the gardeners discovered that field bindweed had crept in among their native plants and infested the garden. "And that's such a major problem; it's almost a case where you need to take out the whole garden, get rid of the field bindweed, and start over again."

Beauregard felt that the Leaside demonstration project offered some important lessons. "To succeed in a team project of this type, one needs three things in equal parts," he said, "expertise, buy-in and commitment." Expertise is important. But without broad buy-in up front — from the community, teachers, students and the school principal — and commitment from dedicated participants to stay with its development over time, a school gardening project is unlikely to succeed.

A brilliantly-coloured damselfly alights in the naturalized pond area.

Exploring in the wildflower and butterfly garden.

FLEMING PUBLIC SCHOOL
Wildflowers and Butterflies

There are few types of gardens as satisfying for schools as a butterfly garden, not only for learning about plant – animal interactions but also for the sheer delight of observation. These gardens have become increasingly popular in school-ground settings, ranging from simple to complex designs and attracting, in all cases, beautiful winged visitors.

The Fleming Public School Wildflower and Butterfly Garden is at the more complex end of the butterfly habitat design. After helping with the planting of eight or nine thousand trees to restore a section of the Rouge Valley watershed adjacent to their school (see chapter 2), the Fleming students and teachers wanted to have a naturalization project right on the school property. In a continuing partnership with their local conservation organization, Friends of the Rouge Watershed (FRW), they participated in the creation of a wildflower-butterfly garden habitat behind their school. FRW staff proposed a design and drew up a list of plant types and species they felt would both echo the natural vegetation of the valley and thrive in a schoolyard setting. They also explained the habitat and benefits to butterflies of the proposed species. Over the winter, the Fleming teachers successfully applied to the Friends of the Environment Foundation of Canada Trust for funding for their project, and by spring FRW staff had prepared a selection of native plants. They also brought tree logs donated by the City of Toronto to lay out a frame for the selected site.

Soil to provide a seven-to-ten-centimetre base was trucked in to smother the existing grass. The underlayer of soil was then topped with a second truckload of fine-grained sand to suppress weed growth. Jim Robb, FRW general manager, supervised the three-day planting event, in which every Fleming student participated. "We divided the kids up into groups of five per Friends of the Rouge Watershed person," he said, "and described to the kids what we were doing, what the plants were, some of the basic botanical information, planting characteristics, a little bit about the soil and why we were doing it. And we worked with them each for about fifteen to twenty minutes. Each child helped to plant a wildflower, at least one each. So there's ownership there."

Fleming students now have a schoolyard habitat where they can observe and learn more about butterflies and insects. "Our kindergarten students did the lifecycle of butterflies," recounted teacher Irene Hodges. "They've been doing it for years, but they've never had a place to put them, and of course it's always a sad day when they have to let the poor butterflies go. But for the last two years it's been wonderful because they're putting them out there in the garden."

Fleming teachers are delighted at the way nature has responded to their efforts. "The number of butterflies coming to the garden is amazing," said Hodges with a smile.

FOREST VALLEY OUTDOOR EDUCATION SCHOOL
Learning in rhythm with the seasons, students mulch the aboriginal garden before winter.

FOREST VALLEY OUTDOOR EDUCATION SCHOOL
A Partnership for Butterflies

A butterfly garden also blooms in the restored green spaces of the Forest Valley Outdoor Education School nestled in the west Don River Valley. Here, the butterfly garden is one of several projects organized by a Naturalization Committee made up of teachers from local schools and from the Forest Valley Outdoor Education School. This partnership brings students and teachers to the outdoor school where they can gain experience in gardening projects and where help is available if needed. Several schools collaborated in creating the butterfly garden. Forest Valley's site manager Sandee Sharpe described some of the steps and participants. "The butterfly garden was our keystone project for 1995–96. This was started by a group of high school kids. They marked and staked out the whole area. Then, in their home schools, they did research on what kind of plants were going to go in the butterfly garden."

Classes from Roywood and Yorkview elementary schools and students from the Adventure Place special needs program joined the project for the planting. As members of the Naturalization Committee, their teachers were able to bring their students for two follow-up visits to Forest Valley to help students increase their sense of ownership in the project. To help the student gardeners maintain an ongoing connection with the butterfly garden, successive visiting classes from their schools check on its progress and report back on how it is doing.

Asked if butterflies are attracted to the plantings and if other students enjoy the garden, Sharpe was unequivocal: "Oh tons! I've taken kindergartens through there to see the butterflies. They find plants that are taller than they are. To be a kindergarten child, and to look up, it's the same feeling that we have when we look up at trees; they're looking up at these plants that are towering over them. To walk through there is marvellous! It's phenomenal."

BENNINGTON HEIGHTS PUBLIC SCHOOL

A Breeding Habitat for Butterflies

At Bennington Heights Public School, tucked away in its corner of East York, parent and landscape architect Debi Rudolph has helped teach the students about interrelationships between plants and animals through the inclusion of butterfly-attracting plants. "I always wanted to add more for the kids to see, to do, to learn about nature around here," she said. Therefore she went beyond simply attracting butterflies and provided them with a breeding habitat as well. "It's one thing to have a butterfly garden as just a nectar garden where you're attracting beneficial insects; most people only do a butterfly garden as mostly nectar. They don't consider the other food stages where you need a food plant. Or the plants that the insects lay the eggs on, or the ones the caterpillars are on. They might not be as wonderful — like stinging nettle, for starters, most people wouldn't want that in their garden — but it's a host plant for the larvae. And grasses, the fact that we have those prairie grasses in there, it's not just for decoration, it's so that they can lay their eggs. A lot of the ones on my wish list are host plants for stuff that I would like to get living there. Because they're good for the caterpillars and they're also good for other bugs."

HUMBERWOOD DOWNS ACADEMY AND FOREST VALLEY OUTDOOR EDUCATION SCHOOL

Living Hedges

Another type of small habitat that has been successfully created by schools is a dual-purpose fence known as a living hedge that can serve simultaneously as a shelter for birds and a child-safety barrier. Humberwood Downs Academy, committed to keeping the schoolyard in harmony with the landscape of the adjacent Humber Valley Conservation Area, chose to plant a living hedge as a safety boundary for the students. This example of a green infrastructure was considered a more attractive and natural addition to the landscape than a traditional chain-link fence. "It's a boundary, but we didn't want a fence," Grade 7 Science teacher Lynn Short declared. "In that living hedge there are things like nannyberry that will make a hedgerow and feed the birds." For the first two years, while the living hedge filled in and matured, a snow fence along the demarcation line of the children's playground provided limits. The project was carried out under the on-going partnership between Humberwood Downs Academy and Humber College.

At Forest Valley Outdoor Education School, there is a similar project that contributes to transforming part of its secluded west Don Valley landscape. "In terms of naturalization, we took out the formal fence all around the playground and said, 'We want to go natural,'" explained Sandee Sharpe. "So one of the fences for the playground is a natural fence. It's brush put between trees. It's called the Living Wall. The students scatter seeds in there as part of their programs; the plants grow up, and all of a sudden we've created habitat for birds!"

Sharpe was emphatic about the number of formal learning opportunities offered by their naturalized areas. "How can it be used? Language and follow-up and reflection. Science and Tech-Characteristics, Needs of Living Things, Growth and Change in Animals, Growth and Change in Plants, Habitats and Communities, studying the habitats and communities by the Living Wall. You can create all of this in your schoolyard!"

FOOD AND HERB GARDENS

As urban dwellers, too many of us have lost direct contact with the miracle of growing food. Canada has become part of a vast, globally linked food production and trading network, weakening urban people's connections with food sources by presenting them with well-designed packages or rows of clean, shiny, beautifully formed fruits and vegetables. This food delivery system offers Canadian families an unprecedented year-round choice in food products from around the world. But it has raised some serious questions about the health and safety of large-scale meat production practices,

SIR ROBERT BORDEN B.T.I.
A space seven by ten metres includes native Ontario plant habitats, a pond and an organic vegetable and herb garden.

composting, pest management without chemicals, growing heritage seeds to protect food species biodiversity and water conservation. They are building a stronger link between people and the working of the earth's natural systems. They are also learning that growing food together builds a sense of community.

chemical applications to crops, the protection of watersheds from agricultural runoff, and the health and environmental effects of genetic engineering and soil exhaustion. Not to mention the cumulative effects on the atmosphere and climate when these food products are moved vast distances by truck or plane.

Contact with growing food is an elemental human experience. In cities around the world, as food production has become distanced from urban centres, there has been a resurgence of interest and participation in local food production. Community food gardens are appearing in parks, on rooftops, in empty lots, in allotment gardens, in hydro corridors — and in schoolyards. The initiators of these projects want to grow fresh vegetables, but they also want to teach and learn about soil and soil enhancement,

Permaculture is a system by which we can exist on the earth by using energy that is naturally in flux and relatively harmless, and by using food and natural resources that are abundant in such a way that we don't continually destroy life on earth. Every technique for conserving and restoring the earth is already known; what is not evident is that any nation or large group of people is prepared to make the change. However, millions of ordinary people are starting to do it themselves.

—BILL MOLLISON,
AN INTRODUCTION TO PERMACULTURE

SIR ROBERT L. BORDEN BUSINESS AND TECHNICAL INSTITUTE

Roosters in the Courtyard

One of the most developed food-growing projects that we encountered in our visits to schools is in the courtyard garden at Sir Robert L. Borden Business and Technical Institute in Scarborough. Science Head John Sherk and his students lovingly brought this oasis of life into being. In a seven-by-ten-metre interior space, they have created an ecologically diverse garden, which includes a pond, a mix of Ontario native plants and habitats and integrated models of sustainable agriculture (more about the pond and its inhabitants can be found later in this chapter). This garden is a living manifestation of Sherk's belief that protection for the natural environment should be part of formal schooling. "The whole point of environmental education is to help people encourage conditions that foster life," he said. "Becoming aware of ourselves as living creatures, the relationships we have with other living creatures, and what living creatures in general depend on for a healthy and happy life and survival is, I think, a very important part of education." Two profound teachings infuse students' experiences in the Borden garden: how healthy ecosystems work and the importance of caring for living things.

Borden's courtyard garden is divided into small-scale mixed fruit, vegetable and herb beds, which are planned and cared for using some of the principles of a sustainable agriculture system called permaculture. "The first part of the permaculture idea is just using what's available," said Sherk, referring to the bags of leaves contributed by neighbours and the school's food-waste collection program that supplies the material for the garden's five composters. The food grown here is organic, meaning that no chemical fertilizers or pesticides are used. "The idea of permaculture is to

SIR ROBERT BORDEN B.T.I.

Chicks raised in the classroom become important members of the garden ecosystems in the courtyard, helping with insect-control and plant fertilization.

produce food using the ecological relationships between the different elements of the garden," Sherk explained. "Actually, the kiwis here are maybe the best example. These are shade-loving kiwis, so they're planted under the flowering crab-apple, using its shade to provide the ideal climate for the kiwis. So I think it's kind of the surprise element for the first time in my life, I've had Ontario-grown kiwis to eat!"

For Sherk's students, gardening is also about learning basic life skills. "I think for a person to take up a lifelong

interest in something can often involve just a little bit of initial exposure to pique their interest and give them a sense of some basic skills. My grade nines all know how to germinate seeds with grow lights, how to transplant them outdoors and how to use compost or leaves as a mulch or as a fertilizer. These kids often are not experienced in the use of hand tools — shovels, garden rakes, clippers, for example. So I've been teaching gardening to them, from germinating the seeds inside to taking care of the plants outdoors." To deal with the ever-present challenge of weeding and watering over the summer, Sherk made an arrangement with a local day-care — it uses the garden in exchange for help with garden maintenance.

An unusual feature of the Borden garden is the inclusion of animals. They form an important part of the energy and nutrient-recycling functions integral to permaculture agriculture systems. Two handsome roosters and a hen raised from chicks by the students strut contentedly around the court-yard, foraging among the plants, reducing insect populations and fertilizing the garden as they go.

The garden is also a setting for formal learning. John Sherk has developed two units for his Grade 10 Science classes that focus on living things in a natural setting. One unit investigates a natural ecosystem, the other investigates the living community in soils. With its lush foliage and a palette of colours, visiting birds and butterflies, tinkling wind chimes and crowing roosters, and the plash of water from the solar-powered waterfall aerating the pond, this courtyard garden is a multi-sensory source of inspiration, exemplifying the feeling of completeness that ecologically diverse surroundings can provide.

JACKMAN AVENUE PUBLIC SCHOOL
Millennium Garden

With the arrival of the year 2000, a group of parents at east-central Toronto's Jackman Avenue Public School felt that adding a garden to their children's schoolyard would be a superb way to celebrate the new millennium. At Jackman, as at many other schools, preliminary inquiries started a buzz of interest in the idea of a garden and brought willing partici-pants together. It also helped to identify the most supportive members of the school administration. "Our principal, Jane Fletcher, is the pillar of our Gardening Committee," parent

---

GARDEN SONG

Pulling weeds, picking stones
We are made of dreams and bones
Need a place to call my own
For the time is near at hand
Grain for grain, sun and rain
Find my way through Nature's chain
Tune my body and my brain
To the music of the land

Inch by inch, row by row
Gonna make this garden grow
All you need is a rake and hoe
And a piece of fertile ground
Inch by inch, row by row
Someone bless these seeds I sow
Someone warm them from below
Till the rains come tumbling down.

© DAVID MALLETT

Summer watering playdays bring parents and children together to care for their millennium garden.

community was so resourceful," remarked Zora Ignatovic, a founding parent. "We made an information table for the spring fair, and people came and were impressed with our idea. We painted a big green thumb on the concrete, and everyone got excited. Everything happened unbelievably well and fast." The plans and the fundraising efforts for Jackman's Millennium Garden progressed rapidly when the Learnxs Foundation provided seed funding. With the arrival of the warm weather, the gardeners were ready to remove 175 square metres of pavement to plant a naturalized area and a food garden, add trees to their playground and build a stone amphitheatre as an outdoor classroom.

The food or teaching garden proved to be a centre of special interest for the young gardeners. "We planted peas, six varieties of beans, corn, squash, tomatoes and some herbs: parsley, thyme, sage, chives," Milne said. "We also planted soup mix to see what we'd get, and to demonstrate that some things in your cupboard are actually seeds that still have the potential to become plants again. It's a good seed project: look in your cupboards and see what you can plant — coriander, soup mix, sunflower seeds, garlic, potatoes, onions." The parents felt strongly about the benefits to children of actively nurturing food as it grew. "The connection between kids and food is very important," emphasized Ignatovich. "Because as long as they don't have a real first-hand experience in growing vegetables, and maybe fruit and herbs, children really don't think about food as a part of the cycles of life: they just take everything from the shelf in the store. I know when I finally picked my first tomato and took a bite it was a wonderful feeling. The smell is different and the taste is different. I believe that kids really can benefit from this experience." Lisa Milne was delighted to see her son both enjoy and grow vegetables. "Kids have a direct understanding of putting seeds in the ground. Seeing what you get, gets kids to eat vegetables, too. Kids who grow vegetables, eat vegetables. My son has eaten his whole harvest!"

Lisa Milne remarked. "Without her, it would be much harder. She has allowed staff to help us with grant applications, and she organized a Garden Club, which meets on Mondays at lunchtime."

During its first winter and spring, the Gardening Committee set out to involve the school community. "Our

For Jackman's new garden, regular maintenance was particularly important during the dry summer months that followed its planting. The Gardening Committee drew up a watering roster, with mothers and their children signing up for each week of summer. Gardening Committee members made their garden a regular meeting place, sharing the chores and enjoying the growing friendships that their project engendered. "We planted all through the summer," remarked Ignatovic. "We wanted to attract people and show them that there was something alive. Everything survived and we were really happy. And in September when the kids came back to school, they were excited."

With the garden established, the Gardening Committee decided that setting up a composting program in the school would provide both an effective waste-reduction method and free soil amendments. Every classroom was provided with a bucket for collecting organic wastes, to be taken out to the composter by one of the students at the end of day. The composting program has significantly reduced the school's food waste.

The garden has also become a new community focus. The mothers have made new friends, the children have had a chance to learn and have fun together as they water the garden — and each other — during watering play-days. The links with living things and with growing food have made a deep impression on all the participants. "As soon as we realize we are part of nature, we have more of a chance to survive," reflected Ignatovic. "It's a nice connection growing there. Our kids are together, and the mothers help each other. It's good to find a space, and recognize where our space is and what our role is inside this complicated system."

JACKMAN AVENUE P.S.
Learning how food grows is one of the miracles of school gardening.

FOREST VALLEY OUTDOOR EDUCATION SCHOOL
An Aboriginal Garden

At Forest Valley Outdoor Education School, the Aboriginal Garden is a unique teaching garden. Site manager Sandee Sharpe briefly explained its evolution: "We started a Native medicine wheel teaching garden, and it evolved into an Aboriginal garden. We have the four sacred plants: sage, sweetgrass, wild tobacco and cedar." This choice of plants is based on Native medicine wheel teachings that honour the four sacred directions; each direction has a specific plant,

animal, culture and life teaching associated with it. Other Native plants known for their medicinal qualities are researched and selected by the students, and species including purple coneflower (from which the popular remedy *Echinacea* is derived) and wild strawberry are planted around the outside of the garden. Sharpe feels that students can benefit greatly from traditional Native teachings. "Much of our medicine doesn't come from a factory or the grocery," she reminds them. "It comes from nature."

BROADACRES PUBLIC SCHOOL
A Heritage Seed Garden

> Professionally and personally, both our livelihoods and our lives depend on the preservation of what we have and the restoration of what we have lost. The fate of farmers — and with them the fate of the earth itself — is not somebody else's problem: it is our fate, too.
>
> — ALICE WATERS,
> *CHEZ PANISSE VEGETABLES*

At Broadacres Public School in Etobicoke, Kathy Caulfield and some of her students are participating in an activity that is becoming increasingly popular among community gardeners: the propagation of heirloom vegetables, fruits, grains, herbs and flowers to preserve genetic biodiversity in domesticated species. Caulfield obtained heritage seeds from Seeds of Diversity Canada, a seed exchange which searches out and preserves traditional and often locally bred plant varieties that are no longer marketed commercially. By growing these types of grains and vegetables, the Broadacres gardeners contribute to a global grassroots effort to maintain the viability of heritage seed stock.

The cultivation of heritage plants offers school gardeners an opportunity to learn about traditional methods used by farmers to select and breed edible varieties of plants that are best suited to their local growing conditions or are resistant to pests. It also enables the gardeners to join with scientists and community gardeners working to preserve these plant varieties bred through many generations of patient selection. Traditional agricultural hybridizing practices can be contrasted with the direction taken by today's massive seed industry: the world's food supply is now based on large-scale, genetically uniform, intensive agriculture in which the use of only a few plant varieties increases crop vulnerability to pests, diseases and environmental stress. One goal of heritage seed saving is the preservation of genetic material that might contribute to the development of new plant varieties capable of tolerating climate change. And there is an additional satisfaction in preserving the viability of locally bred plant varieties: gardeners growing heritage seeds often discover that their heritage crops have the advantage of being hardier than many commercial species — as well as being very delicious!

POND AND BOG GARDENS

> Water, lifeblood of all living beings, has long held a hallowed place within the human spirit.
>
> — JEAN-MARC DAIGLE AND DONNA
> HAVINGA, *RESTORING NATURE'S PLACE:*
> *A GUIDE TO NATURALIZING ONTARIO*
> *PARKS AND GREENSPACE*

An opportunity for contact with an aquatic ecosystem can offer students a special first-hand exposure to the intricate interplay of earth, air and water — both a scientific and a profoundly personal experience of the mysteries of nature. Besides adding beauty and interest to a school setting, ponds and bogs offer unique potential for teaching young people about the importance of protecting Ontario's precious freshwater ecosystems. Across formal subject areas, studies of living water environments can also give students a taste of the many interconnections among soil, temperature, water, gravity, plant and animal forms, chemistry, hydrology, geology, the cycling of water and nutrients, food chains, photosynthesis and local biodiversity.

ANSON S. TAYLOR PUBLIC SCHOOL
A Pond Between the Wings

Two years after the staff and students of Anson S. Taylor Public School in Scarborough had begun their transformation of the V-shaped outdoor space between the two wings of their school building into a naturalized area, they recognized

ANSON S. TAYLOR P.S.

Nature moves into a school pond: sedges and rushes grow well in miniature wetland ecosystems.

Their inquiries took them to conservation areas and to other schools. They also contacted the Toronto Zoo and studied its information on the Adopt-a-Pond program. "I used the Adopt-a-Pond curriculum guide," says Weissman of her early research efforts, "and zoo staff gave us a lot of advice about what species to plant." The principal expressed some concerns about safety, which were allayed by Weissman's thorough investigation into successful pond-building projects. He then became a strong ally in obtaining necessary approvals from school board authorities. One concern, for example, was the safety of children around a pond. Weissman and her students discovered that one of the safety regulations for pond-building stipulated that if a pond were deeper than forty-five centimetres, it would need to have a fence around it. "I would not advise anyone to initiate a project without support from the principal," noted Weissman. "You must have support from the administration."

With funding in hand, pond-building plans moved ahead. Each stage of Anson S. Taylor's project was a learning experience for the students involved. "We used the prices and quantities of tools and equipment for the pond to practise Math," recalled Weissman. "And we did measurement activities on volume and capacity when the holes were being dug." As they had sufficient room on the site, the Anson S. Taylor gardeners decided to add a second pond. The students helped with the design, using triangulation techniques to take the measurements and draw up plans. Additional private funding enabled the purchasing of computer resources and books to help the students enhance their outdoor experience with formal classroom learning on the diversity of living things.

Weissman and school audio-visual staff member Cheryl Fitzpatrick produced two videos of the entire pond-building and planting process, with scripts written and narrated by participating students. They also made new contacts as they added living things to their ponds. "We had a wonderful

ANSON S. TAYLOR P.S.
Caring for naturalized school ponds includes removing excess algae, duckweed and overgrowth of grasses and rushes.

that a pond would greatly complement their existing trees and perennials. Renay Weissman, then a Grade 5 teacher, set out with her class to research pond-building. They began by visiting wetlands and ponds, both natural and constructed.

herpetologist named Margaret Boat, who has a collection of many reptiles," Weissman said. "She brought Peaches the snake to visit, and she takes care of our turtles over the summer." Former Scarborough Assistant Co-ordinator of Outdoor and Environmental Education Ken Andrews played a key role in facilitating contacts among schools engaged in naturalization projects. "He was really, really helpful," remembered Weissman of his support of several schools undertaking aquatic ecosystem projects. "We had habitat restoration workshops. I went to several professional development days where I shared what we were doing, which helped other people and got them interested." The former Scarborough Board of Education was a pioneer in advancing the building of ponds on school property, paying particular attention to safety issues. It set the maximum depth at forty-five centimeters, and provided advice and assistance to teachers on how to select emergent plants that would grow into an aquatic habitat and attract small creatures but not wading children.

A pair of mallard ducks arrives every spring to settle on the two secluded ponds tucked between the wings of the school. The reeds and other aquatic plants there are also home to frogs, toads, damselflies and dragonflies. Through their classroom windows, the students can watch the birds that visit their own piece of restored nature year round. Renay Weissman and all the Anson S. Taylor staff are committed to making contact with nature an integral part of education at their school.

Renay Weissman sums up their philosophy on the inter-disciplinary approach to teaching students through the natural environment: "Anything they're never going to forget has to mean something on many levels of their being."

SATEC@W.A. PORTER C.I.

Science students collect water samples for comparative water tests.

SATEC@W.A. PORTER COLLEGIATE INSTITUTE
Adding New Dimensions to Learning

When W.A. Porter Collegiate Institute in Scarborough elected to add a new dimension to its programs to attract students, it chose the environment. Science Head Michelle Barraclough took on the responsibility of co-ordinating the school's new focus. She worked with staff and outside environmental educators and consultants to develop a vision of what an environmental school would look like inside and outside, how things would change and how the environment could be implemented in the curriculum. The new environmental focus eventually led to the creation of the Scarborough Academy for Technical, Environmental and Computer Education, or *satec@W.A. Porter.*

Early in the process of developing environmental programs and activities, school-ground naturalization became a part of the planning. And from the beginning Barraclough felt that a pond would be an important natural feature to include in ecological landscaping efforts. A visit to Renay Weissman at Anson S. Taylor Public School provided both the inspiration and the practical contacts to begin work on a pond at *satec*. The rest was organization, teamwork and fundraising.

"Each week during my prep I would take out one or two classes to work on something that had to do with it," explained Barraclough. "It was all grass to start with. We dug up the grass and the sod, and underneath it was all clay, hard as a rock. After that the grounds staff used a rototil, so that made it a little bit easier." When the site was prepared, grounds staff arrived with digging equipment to dig the hole. "The owner of our local nursery generously came and showed us how to put the liner down. The kids and I did the rest. The staff here was great: they all came out and helped. Basically the entire school was involved in putting it all together."

The new pond was lined with soil and landscaped with large decorative rocks around its perimeter. It proved to be fertile ground for a vigorous growth of aquatic plants: native lilies, arrowheads, marsh marigolds and grasses thrive in its waters, while its edges bloom with irises, snowflake, dogwood, serviceberry and beautiful native loosestrife. And not only is it beautiful, it has also become a site to inspire budding scientists.

Michelle Barraclough described some of her class activities involving the pond: "We mostly use it for grades ten and eleven Science. With the grade elevens, we used the pond to do water testing, and we

SATEC@W.A.PORTER C.I.
Students research water problems that affect local watersheds as part of pond and stream studies.

took them to do stream studies with Centennial College. They practised on the pond, then they'd go down to Taylor/Massey Creek and do stream studies. I also had a project last year where they chose what they wanted to do, composting or precipitation. They could look at water and test the soil or the water, and give us data on it. The other part of the research assignment was to find some type of water problem that either exists today or existed fairly recently. One was the Oak Ridges Moraine. I also occasionally use the pond in OAC Biology, when we do some of the studies outside. And I think the photography department uses it when they send the kids outside to take pictures."

At *satec*, teachers witnessed a shift in the attitudes of students who worked in the outdoor setting. "I found they were a bit more ethical. I know with my grade ten class, when we started off, it was 'Do we have to do this, Miss?'" noted Barraclough. "What I do with my grade tens is I give them a plant, and I say, 'This is *your* plant.' They start to look after it, and then it's 'Is my plant okay, Miss?'"

Why, despite the extra effort required in a busy schedule, does Michelle Barraclough feel that contact with living things is especially important for students in a technologically focused school? "I think because these students spend so much time on computers, they need to get out and do something else. The kids still get really excited when they see those little seedlings come out of the ground. I think they need the connection to life. As adults, if they're making decisions that have some effect on life, then I want them to know and at least consider the possible outcomes of any decision they make. That's why."

SIR ROBERT BORDEN B.T.I.

Enjoying the luxuriant flowers of the butterfly bush.

SIR ROBERT L. BORDEN BUSINESS AND TECHNICAL INSTITUTE
A Living Aquatic System

The central courtyard at Sir Robert L. Borden Business and Technical Institute is a feast of botanical diversity for the eyes — and for the soul, Science Head John Sherk might add. At the heart of this peaceful green space — amid butterfly bushes, a thicket to attract birds, native woodland plants, fragrant herbs, an organic vegetable garden and the contented cluckings of glossy-feathered roosters and chickens — is a pond

SATEC@W.A.
PORTER C.I.

*Water plantain and
duckweed thrive in
the peace water
garden pond.*

things. "I love it when the kids find a toad!" he smiled. The pond has become home to some other creatures, as well as providing a place for honing observational skills. "There's all kinds of interesting stuff in the pond — water striders, dragonflies, dragonfly nymphs, and a lot of different aquatic insects in different stages of insect life."

The pond's living aquatic system is also an in-house source of samples for water and soil testing by Science classes learning to use microscopes. Sherk integrates work and observation in his outdoor classroom with formal learning in his Science laboratories: "Students take a sample — pond water or soil — upstairs and use either the stereo microscopes at low magnification or the compound microscopes."

Borden's solar pump keeps its pond water well aerated, but there is a need for maintenance to keep plant growth under control. "The water's definitely clean," said Sherk, "but we do have some trouble with the duckweed growing excessively. The algae isn't so much of a problem — we just pull it out from time to time, reducing it to a quarter of what it was, and let it grow back."

John Sherk notices a feeling of ownership on the part of his students towards their garden. Some of them volunteer to help with maintenance, and he finds a quiet satisfaction in watching them care for the living things that they have helped to grow together. "I remember ... when we came to clean out the pond, this kid was right in there with his waders on, lifting out the pond plants that needed to be brought out. With this class, there is just a real sense of their own pleasure in doing it."

with a gently splashing solar-powered water system. "We put in the pond because I felt that it was really important in connection with the bird habitat to attract birds. Birds need water. It's also important to us, just to make it a more interesting place," explained Sherk.

He and a colleague worked with their classes to install and plant the pond. Its first inhabitants were American toad tadpoles. "We were advised by the Toronto Zoo that one shouldn't just move adult toads from one section of the neighbourhood to another," recalled Sherk. "I went down one morning and caught tadpoles from about a billion that were swimming in the Chester Springs Marsh, and brought them back and put them in the pond. Fortunately a few of them survived to reproduce here. We brought some sand in, because for the toads you have to have a wintering-over area where they can dig in." Sherk takes great pleasure in encouraging his students to cultivate an appreciation for living

BROADACRES PUBLIC SCHOOL

Striking a Balance with Nature

But all is not always peaceful in nature's kingdom. This was perhaps one of the more surprising lessons learned when the teachers and students at Broadacres Public School installed a pond in their school's courtyard. Soon after its completion, they were delighted to see a pair of mallard ducks move into their small, well-sheltered water hole. Their excitement increased when the pair produced a family of ducklings right outside their windows. Their pleasure was to be short-lived, however, when more adult mallards appeared. Evidently anxious to secure a breeding space for their own families, the new arrivals began to attack the young of the original couple.

The teachers contacted members of the hunting and conservation organization Ducks Unlimited to ask for advice: their suggestion was to make all the ducks leave and settle elsewhere. Teacher Kathy Caulfield recalled their attempts to discourage their tumultuous tenants. "Ducks Unlimited suggested netting the pond. The ducks wouldn't leave. We tried police tape, but the ducks flew under it. Then we converted the pond to a bog and filled it with peat. My grade four class, as part of their studies on the preservation of wetlands, helped plant the bog. The rain keeps the bog moist enough to support wetland plants." As a result, the ducks moved on.

Despite Broadacres's need to settle the duck dispute by converting their pond to a bog, the enthusiasm with which the two families of birds adopted this small piece of restored nature serves as an illustration of how nature will respond to human efforts to provide wildlife habitat. Striking a new balance between human activity and nature's place will be a pivotal challenge of the twenty-first century in which schools must play an important role.

chapter *4*   T O U C H   T H E   E A R T H
L A N D S C A P E S   F O R   A C T I V E   P L A Y

If your school grounds are nothing but barren rectangles of hard surfaces and pounded grass, perhaps it is time to take a closer look at the options for changing your children's living and learning environments and for de-paving the way to a better and more hopeful future.

> — Ann Coffey, "Transforming School Grounds," in *Greening School Grounds: Creating Habitats for Learning*

The many benefits to students of regular contact with natural environments continue to be documented in educational studies in the United Kingdom, the United States and Canada. The findings repeatedly confirm that exposure to naturalized landscapes makes a noticeable difference in the quality of children's school experiences.[8] It is just such regular exposure that some teachers and parents seek to provide for children when they design landscapes for active play. Compared with discrete gardens (which are mainly patches of carefully tended plants where children are only allowed to venture while they are planting, weeding or using the area for a specific formal learning activity), gardens and landscapes for active play are designed to provide shade, shelter, visual interest and variety while withstanding the daily onslaught of happy active children during free time.

All of the elements — trees, shrubs and flowering plants — in these *activity gardens* are selected for their hardy qualities. The landscape, arranged to provide pathways and seating areas that allow children freedom of movement,

offers four advantages that, as many parents and teachers recognize, are important to young children. One, of course, is shade protection, particularly critical at midday in the warm fall, spring and summer months. A second is shelter from the heat in summer and wind in winter. A third, in this textured space, is an invitation to games of imagination, hiding, chasing and make-believe. A fourth is a variety of small-scale sheltered places of refuge for quiet play and small-group gatherings, a welcome change for some children from the larger, more open paved playgrounds.

In addition, landscapes for active play offer children numerous opportunities to learn. Participation in planting, and even assistance with design, give children a tremendous sense of pride and ownership in "their" play garden. Large trees may require planting by grounds staff, but smaller trees, shrubs and flowering plants can be set in by the very students for whom these activity gardens are intended. For young gardeners, routine maintenance, mulching, weeding, pruning and cleanups help develop a sense of responsibility and shared stewardship for a place that grows with them.

BROADACRES PUBLIC SCHOOL
A Field Garden

Broadacres Public School's field garden is an outstanding example of a landscape for active play. This project evolved through several stages of landscaping. It began with a simple decision by some of the school's teachers to plant three trees on the barren pavement-dirt-and-grass playing field to create

some shade and shelter for the children. It became apparent soon afterwards, however, that the soil around the trees was becoming compacted by the regular tramping of children at play. The teachers decided to add native shrubs to protect the trees, a process that began the ongoing expansion of the natural landscaping surrounding the playing field. When in successive years the Broadacres Naturalization Committee decided to plant native Carolinian species of trees and under-storey plants, they recognized that the new sections of the garden should be planted in berms, or mounded earth, to reduce soil compaction. They selected each new addition to reflect native species in the community; these species were hardy and drought- and heat-tolerant to enhance their likelihood of survival, keep maintenance to a manageable level and enable the garden to become a more or less self-sustaining model of habitat rehabilitation.

An exceptional feature of Broadacres's field garden is the involvement of the children in its layout and design. "The idea came from the children," said Kathy Caulfield, chair-person of the Naturalization Committee. "They wanted a maze they could run in and around. They helped create it, and we've allowed it to happen because we thought it was a worthwhile activity." The students drew their play garden as a maze, using hoses and skipping ropes to mark out the actual space. After that, the final design was drawn up by the Committee, made up of teachers and a group of parent volunteers. "There are little quiet spaces within the garden, where they can go between the shrubs, away from the hustle and bustle," Caulfield added.

The field garden, the courtyard garden and the swale (or naturalized meadow) are maintained through school community efforts. Volunteers participate in a spring and a fall work day, and in two summer weeding parties. To show their appreciation for their summer volunteer help, the Committee offers participants breakfast in the cool morning hours. During the warm school months, teacher Linda

Kulesha runs a garbage challenge for the students to keep the gardens tidy, and a plantain challenge to keep the weeds under control. Once a week at lunchtime, the Broadacres Nature Club meets. Any child in the school is welcome to join in the effort to keep the sections of the school's gardens clean, weeded and beautiful.

Teacher Janice Harper described one ingenious method developed at Broadacres for helping students learn the names of their native trees. "We had Carolinian trees, and no one knew what they were, including me! So we played a 'tree detective game' with an integrated unit of Science, Math and Art. We had the kids go out and find four characteristics of each tree, describe them, draw them and write about them using various writing forms. It's a guessing game. They'd give four characteristics, and write these in a booklet. Looking at the characteristics, the descriptors and the pictures, you had to identify the name of the tree from the children's information from all these criteria." The teachers ran the tree detective game at recess, involving the entire school, one class at a time. There was a ballot box and a prize at the end of the game, and Broadacres's students emerged victorious and tree-literate.

MAURICE CODY PUBLIC SCHOOL
A Discovery Garden

Some of the parents at Maurice Cody Public School in mid-town Toronto agreed that their children's school playground was definitely not as pleasing as they might have liked. The idea of creating a school garden arose in a response to this simple observation. Carol-Ann Coulter and a small group of fellow parents set out to find some advice on how they could beautify their children's play environment. They consulted Margery Winkler, another Cody parent, who was at the time director of the Landscape Architecture department at Toronto's Ryerson Polytechnic University. Her advice came as something of a surprise: "Don't just garden to beautify," she told them, "make an ecosystem. Relate the parts to the whole. Ask how your school is connected to the world, and how does everything else relate?"

Greening a school, the parents discovered, can include far more than making the grounds look pretty. For Coulter and the other Maurice Cody parents, it was the beginning of a quest. "We read everything we could," she said. They contacted Evergreen and Greensaver, local environmental groups, for advice and guidance. Then they sought the help of their area school community advisor in organizing a planning workshop. She asked them important questions. "What do you want? What do you want to see happen in five years?"

The members of the Ecosystem Committee, as the parents elected to name their garden group, invited students from Ryerson Polytechnic University to visit the school to find out what everybody wanted. What did the students think greening a school might include? Everyone had ideas. Everyone offered suggestions on how their schoolyard might change. The parents gathered the school's collective aspirations and set out to create a gardening plan.

After several proposed drafts, the committee presented a three-part plan for the Discovery Garden, which included a Spiral Garden, a Carolinian woodland meadow and a shaded stone seating area named the Council Ring. Further modifications, with helpful suggestions from grounds staff expert Bruce Day, brought the plan closer to reality. "Bruce will move mountains," Coulter observed. "He cares above all for the grounds."

The Discovery Garden is located behind the school, between a paved play area and a grassy field. The parents felt it was important for the garden to be in a central location to make it easy for the children to both work and play there. The Spiral Garden is made up of a series of small classroom plots connected by a winding path that creates an interesting maze-like pattern. "We each have our own plot in it,"

MAURICE CODY P.S.

Hands-on learning about sunflowers, native to North America since 3000 B.C., in the discovery garden.

*TERRAVIEW–
WILLOWFIELD P.S.*
**The infinite variety of
nature: a popular theme
for the creation of art
projects.**

designed to be adaptable to play time, gardening time and formal learning.

"When I first came to Maurice Cody I was spellbound by the garden," said Carter. "I thought it was fabulous. I've really enjoyed using it myself, and I am very impressed by the degree of parent involvement. Whereas the Spiral Garden is whatever we decide, a butterfly garden or a mixture, the Council Ring isn't really a garden. It's a circle of rocks set underneath the pine trees, a large and lovely meeting place, but the children actually end up playing games or jumping from rock to rock. And it's also a good area for storytelling in the shade."

This landscape for active play is also a learning ground for the students at Maurice Cody. Cindy English is a parent who has been instrumental in the garden's success over the years. "The garden has made an incredible difference for us and for the community at large. People never knew what a Carolinian forest was until they found what species we had here. We've learned about the Carolinian deciduous forest from Lake Erie to Toronto, all the way down the Appalachians to the Carolinas. We get the smallest number of frost days, and have the largest amount of biodiversity anywhere in Canada. With endangered species as part of our program, the whole idea is that it starts in the garden, and we spread it through the community so that eventually we can link all the way across Lake Ontario. We're concentrating on endangered species in our backyard, not in Brazil. And we've learned that the school is part of the Cudmore Creek watershed, one of Toronto's 'lost' rivers.

"The kids now know turtleheads and black-eyed Susans. We watch the bees go inside the petals of the turtleheads. It's a magical, mystical experience, just sitting here watching the bees — thousands! And the colours and the sunflowers are wonderful. People walk through the neighbourhood and through the park and the schoolyard who never had any reason to walk there before, lots of seniors, who say 'Hello,

explained Grade 3 teacher Clare Carter, "so each class has about a one-and-a-half metre area within the spiral. The Spiral Garden has a huge rock in the centre that collects water; you can put your finger in it and draw on the rock; it's kind of a magical place." The adjoining woodland meadow was designed as a native ecosystem restoration effort, and is surrounded by stumps laced together with rope to allow for climbing activities while protecting the vegetation. The entire area is an integral part of the school's playground, and what gorgeous flowers, we had to come and see!' We have goldfinches in the trees, in the scotch pine, everywhere!"

Caring for this space, which combines formal and informal activity in one naturalized landscape, is a work of love taken on by the parents, the teachers who adopt individual garden plots and the Garden Guardians parent volunteers who go out at recess with a big carry-box and ask student volunteers to help them. They recruit the students for a variety of garden activities that Carter described as increasing their "awareness of nature, of life, of beauty." They have also organized older students (Grades 4, 5, 6) to conduct spring garden tours with classes, parents and visitors — they have even had delegates from the United States — through the different gardens.

The parent volunteers developed an ingenious system for rotating garden care, assigning each class one maintenance week in the garden at a time. The parents give each caretaking class a journal in which to record its work. The students borrow the gardening tools from the basement, and as they work, they write down whatever they do in their own garden plots or in the whole garden in general — cleaning up litter, weeding, watering — or anything of interest they see.

Besides teamwork, learning and active play, the Maurice Cody garden provides aesthetic delights. "It's lovely to be out of the classroom!" Carter exclaimed. "When we did our

BROADACRES P.S.

Soft surfaces, logs for balancing and sitting, and green bowers of naturalized space offer children new possibilities for active play.

sketching, I told the children to pretend they were magnifying glasses: 'Actually look, *look* at all the little things. When you draw a flower, it isn't a kindergarten flower any more. Take a look at it. It's got veins, and hair, and little things all over it.' They really were silent, they looked, they watched and they came back with some beautiful detailed drawings. But if they hadn't thought about it … they would have had a different way of seeing it."

chapter 5 BRINGING NATURE TO SCHOOL

HABITAT REHABILITATION PROJECTS

This is the first time in the history of human experience on this earth that we're rebuilding natural landscapes. We've never done this before.

— HENRY KOCK,
INTERPRETIVE HORTICULTURALIST,
GUELPH ARBORETUM

BRINGING NATURE into the school experience is a dynamic way of establishing a new and vital link with what the provincial curriculum calls "the world outside the school." An important part of the school-ground gardening movement is the restoration of habitat for local species that have been displaced by urban development and agriculture. But schools involved in habitat rehabilitation as an educational activity are doing far more than simply greening their landscapes or providing homes for native plants, birds, butterflies and small wildlife. They are restoring a lost aspect of their own place, and creating spaces where the vital processes of nature can resume in the midst of human settlement. By paying attention to natural systems in their own particular geographical location, and coming to understand nature's own restorative processes of natural succession close at hand, students share in the work of preserving ecosystem health.

Habitat rehabilitation projects on school grounds offer students many opportunities to learn. From an educational perspective, these projects quite naturally invite a multi-disciplinary approach to their planning and development.

Becoming involved in the restoration of even a small corner of a schoolyard to its natural state invites students to investigate their area's local history, geography, watershed and species. It also gives them experience in small-scale land-use planning, from envisioning how the landscape will be transformed to mapping, measuring, drafting plans and drawing to scale.

As a new area of learning for most educators, involvement in restoration projects offers the rewarding prospect of connecting their students to the broader community. Collaboration with landscape architects, conservationists, horticulturists, naturalists and environmentalists can open up a new world of ecological knowledge to students whose lives are separated from the natural world by urban living and the pervasiveness of modern technologies. Involvement in naturalization projects can be, for many young people, a way to learn about native plants in their local environments — an important step towards seeing and valuing their own place in a new way. This new understanding, in other words, can enable students to develop a strong sense of stewardship.

NATURAL SUCCESSION

The potential for developing naturalized landscapes requires us to look at the way nature deals with degraded landscapes. It is useful to understand something of nature's processes if we wish to mimic them.

Ontario is divided by its major ecosystems into four life zones: the Carolinian, the Great Lakes – St. Lawrence, the Boreal and the Tundra. A narrow band of Ontario's "deep south," including the Toronto area and the northwest shore of Lake Ontario, falls within the most northerly reaches of the Carolinian zone. This zone, which extends south to the American Carolinas (from which it takes its name), is one of the most biologically diverse in Canada. But because of its high human population densities, it also contains some of the most fragmented natural habitat in Canada. Most of Ontario's endangered species live within the remnant vegetation of the Carolinian zone. For school communities, therefore, living in this area represents a rich opportunity to become active participants in the preservation of flora and fauna whose habitats have been displaced by human activity.

Ecologists refer to any space where vegetation has been removed and natural processes interrupted as a "disturbance." Fires, floods and other natural disasters create disturbances by stripping landscapes. Human development creates disturbances wherever vegetation is removed and replaced by buildings, pavement and human-cultivated plants: in these places, nature can no longer thrive in its own way. Cities, therefore, are ecological disturbances.

Nature has a fascinating dynamic process called *natural succession*, through which living landscapes renew themselves after a disturbance. In a simplified model of forest succession, there is a somewhat predictable sequence of vegetation growth. Within a period of one hundred to three hundred years, each sequence prepares the site for the establishment of the next sequence through a succession of changing conditions. As different kinds of plants move in and establish themselves in the former clearing, they change it: they create shade, add nutrients to the soil, help the soil retain moisture and alter the temperature patterns, producing new patterns of vegetation and new plant communities.

In a barren space, the first species to arrive are short-lived herbaceous plants (often referred to as "forbs," short for flowering herbs), whose seeds may have remained dormant in the soil or been dispersed to the site by wind or wildlife. These are the hardy little plants most people refer to as weeds. Gradually, longer-lived perennial herbs and grasses overtake them, and the area becomes a grassy meadow. These pioneering species do the important work of stabilizing and reconditioning depleted soils, preparing them for future growth. In nature, this phase may last anywhere from ten to twenty-five years. A common problem at this pioneering stage, particularly in ecologically degraded urban landscapes, can be the invasion — and sometimes dominance — of non-native species whose aggressive growth may influence the course of natural succession by out-competing native species.

Once a meadow is established, shrubs, vines and trees gradually overtake the herbaceous plant community as the area evolves into what is called the "woody pioneer" stage. Over a twenty-five to fifty year period, these woody plants completely shade out the meadow, adding layers of leaves and other organic debris to build up the topsoil further. During this stage, longer-lived species such as oak, red and sugar maples, elm and white pine often appear among the shorter-lived softwood trees such as poplar and birch.

During the next twenty-five to fifty years, as the more durable species of shrubs and trees mature, the woody pioneer stage moves into a "mature forest" stage. The trees grow taller and fill out to provide a denser, shadier canopy above an understorey of shade-tolerant shrubs such as serviceberry, dogwood, hazelnut, mountain maple and raspberry. The final phase in forest succession, which can take another fifty to 150 years to achieve, is called the "climax," or "old growth," stage. Longer-lived, shade-tolerant species fill in the understorey beneath a canopy of tall, mature trees.

Historically, the old-growth forests of southern Ontario contained trees of all ages and sizes, with tall pines protruding through a nearly continuous ceiling of mature trees, and smaller trees and shrubs growing in the understorey. Periodic disturbances, both large and small, opened up gaps in the forest canopy, letting in sunlight to stimulate growth and renewal and provide the conditions required to maintain diversity. Dead trees offered homes for many species of birds and small animals; decaying branches and leaf litter on the forest floor created habitat for fungi, reptiles, amphibians, invertebrates and bacteria. The biodiversity of our historic southern old-growth forests can provide inspiration today for our own contemporary efforts at habitat rehabilitation.

FOREST VALLEY OUTDOOR EDUCATION SCHOOL

Measuring, monitoring, and keeping records of growth and change in restored natural areas.

GRASSLAND ECOSYSTEMS

The term *habitat rehabilitation* often brings to mind an image of landscapes restored through the planting of trees and shrubs. But another, less well recognized but no less important part of our landscape is its wild open spaces: meadows, tall grass prairies and other grassland ecosystems. It is estimated that Ontario once had as many as one thousand square kilometres of tall grass prairies, of which less than 3 percent remains today. This prairie ecosystem once included over two hundred species of plants such as berg-amot and blazing-star, and teemed with a variety of wildlife — birds such as bobolinks, northern bobwhite quail and savannah sparrows, and mammals such as deer, voles and badgers. The plants and animals of this landscape were more typical of the American Midwest than of the Ontario forest. The Toronto region's largest prairies were located around the eastern Beaches and the Scarborough Bluffs, and on the river

**When we garden,
we may be escaping into a world
we've created with care and labour and
seeds and water and vision, but
we are also participating in and
connecting with something beyond
ourselves; we are nurturing life.**

— LORRAINE JOHNSON,
*TENDING THE EARTH:
A GARDENER'S MANIFESTO*

HUMBERWOOD DOWNS ACADEMY

Classified as an Environmentally Sensitive Area (ESA), this marshy meadow gives the school both a share in responsibility for its protection and a chance to learn from its ecosystems.

bluffs along the Credit and Rouge Rivers. These dry sandy plains maintained their open character through frequent ground fires, often started by lightning strikes. Interpretive horticulturalist Henry Kock, a champion of the restoration of Ontario's wild meadows, advises would-be restorers of natural spaces to "get beyond the temptation to plant all open areas full of trees." Ontario's native prairies need as much protection as its forests.

Growing awareness of the biodiversity present in grassland ecosystems has prompted interest in restoring wildflower meadows and tall grass prairies as ecologically sound substitutes for more traditional and higher maintenance turf-grass lawns. With proper management, varied expanses of native grasses and wildflowers can become attractive, low-maintenance substitutes for lawns. Native grassland ecosystems are species-rich and drought-tolerant, which vary throughout the seasons and support numerous bird, mammal, insect and butterfly species. In urbanized areas, where development has fragmented or removed the former natural landscape, restored grassland ecosystems can provide an important place of refuge for species whose populations have dwindled as a result of lost habitat.

GIVING NATURE A HAND

Once they are removed, ecosystems cannot be replaced in their original form by human design. Particular environments do, however, tend to give rise to certain kinds and patterns of vegetation characteristic of these ecosystems. Restoration efforts, or *enhanced natural succession*, in degraded places can give new plant communities a head start and boost their regenerative momentum over time. Habitat rehabilitation efforts cannot ensure that a new plant community will become as complex as a natural community, which may have taken hundreds — or even thousands — of years to evolve. However, a human-initiated plant

PRAIRIES OR MEADOWS:
WHAT'S THE DIFFERENCE?

In contemplating the naturalization of open spaces, it is useful to note the difference between meadows and prairies. A meadow is usually the product of a forest disturbance (we should remember that despite present appearances, most of Ontario was once forest land). It is therefore a temporary, successional plant community that, if left undisturbed, will eventually revert to forest. A prairie, on the other hand, is an old-growth grassland community. Prairies tend to grow in areas where, for lack of moisture, forests cannot. Before colonization, tall grass prairies and black oak savannahs were quite common in southwestern Ontario; they are now rare and endangered communities, growing primarily in small areas that have escaped the advances of agriculture and urbanization.

community can stimulate natural processes to take root and flourish, so that revegetated areas can evolve according to new patterns of succession.

In schoolyards or other severely degraded sites where there is limited vegetation, enhanced succession begins with a decision about what kind of ecosystem restoration is most appropriate and desirable: forest, wetland, meadow or prairie. Each ecosystem type must then be analyzed in terms of the community of plant species that grow and co-exist naturally in the local area or bioregion. From this first list (or "plant community model"), native plants that are locally available for restoring a selected site are chosen. Choosing a mix of the hardiest, most resilient native species that mimic natural plant communities increases the likelihood of the successful establishment of a new plant community that can withstand a variety of soil types and moisture conditions.

*

How then, have schools approached habitat rehabilitation? Across Toronto there are many exciting examples of habitat rehabilitation that demonstrate the different types of projects undertaken and the learning opportunities that accompany them. In Scarborough, Terraview-Willowfield Public School has joined with its community and the local conservation authority in revegetating a transformed aquatic landscape as part of an effort to rehabilitate their local tributary of the Don River. In the west end of the city, at Humberwood Downs Academy, students have naturalized a marshy meadow that borders on the Humber Arboretum conservation lands. In Etobicoke, Broadacres Public School has rehabilitated a swale, a grassy meadowland restoration where foxes and killdeer have been seen. In

FOREST VALLEY OUTDOOR EDUCATION SCHOOL
Three-bin composting reduces school waste and offers a detailed lesson on how nature converts organic matter into biologically-stable free home-made fertilizer.

east-central Toronto, Eastdale Collegiate has created winding paths through their Woodland Garden, a new bower of native vegetation in the middle of a busy urban neighbourhood. In west-central Toronto, Runnymede Public School has spent nearly ten years nurturing a nature-study garden that echoes the larger scale naturalization of neighbouring High Park, and Ranchdale Public School's Naturalization Club is rehabilitating an area in North York by planting birch trees students grew from seedlings. In addition, two of Toronto's outdoor education schools have been helping teachers and students learn about Ontario's ecosystems and the importance of restoring natural areas.

TERRAVIEW-WILLOWFIELD PUBLIC SCHOOL
Restoring a Waterway

I've had occasion to come in on the weekend, and I can remember a couple of times last winter particularly where you looked out and it looked like a postcard. You sort of got a lump in your throat because it had snowed. Somebody had cleared the snow. There were mums and kids skating. There were a couple of kids with hockey sticks. It was breathtaking. It was beautiful.

— BARBARA SHERIFF-SCOTT, PRINCIPAL, TERRAVIEW-WILLOWFIELD PUBLIC SCHOOL

Terraview-Willowfield Public School is located in the valley of the historic Taylor/Massey Creek, a sub-watershed of Toronto's Don River. The area through which this creek flows has been heavily urbanized: the creek itself is barely recognizable as a river in its upper reaches, having been piped into or confined in concrete channels over much of its length. In 1992, the Don Watershed Task Force was created to develop a regeneration plan for the entire Don River, using an ecosystem approach. Their vision for the watershed's future was expressed in a three-part mandate: "To protect what is healthy, to regenerate what is degraded and to take responsibility for the Don."

Heavily used as a storm drain and a sewer, and stripped of nearly all of its natural vegetation, Taylor/Massey Creek has the dubious distinction of being the most degraded of the main tributaries of the Don watershed. The challenge, therefore, for the communities along its length is to join forces to restore it to a clean, healthy natural waterway. The students of Terraview-Willowfield Public School have had the privilege of being a part of this ambitious transformation first-hand, literally in their own yard: Taylor/Massey Creek flows right outside the school's front door.

The project to regenerate the creek and transform the playing field facing Terraview-Willowfield into a naturalized pond habitat began in 1993. "There was a lot of consultation — community members, politicians, parents — the school was represented by the principal at the time, a staff member and a trustee, and the city had a Parks person present," principal Barbara Sheriff-Scott noted. "There was discussion around two elements — doing something with the watershed and doing something with the creek. Parents were concerned about having a concrete catchment basin with almost no water in the summer, and then during a rainy period — within minutes — having a metre-ful of rushing water. It presented quite a safety hazard to children. And people were interested in a park that had more resources, more facilities, and paths and walkways."

After five years of community planning, a proposal for the rehabilitation of the section adjoining the school was completed with the restoration work being divided into two phases. The concrete culvert was removed and the creek was rerouted to make a more natural, gently curving streambed. Teacher Alison Luck described the help offered by the experts, "The Parks people chose the trees. They knew what kind of trees would survive best, and they planned the actual layout." When the plan was ready, word went out to the entire community that help was needed with the work of relandscaping the banks of the newly naturalized creek. The goal of Phase One was to plant native plants to naturalize the more northerly section of the creek banks.

"In Phase One," related Ms. Luck, "there was a community planting day on a Saturday where everyone came out; parents came as volunteers. There was another planting on a school day, and the students helped plant the trees. We

TERRAVIEW–WILLOWFIELD P.S.

Taylor/Massey Creek, formerly a degraded branch of the Don River, once again wanders though a winter landscape, returning to health after years of co-operative community effort that included parks staff, neighbours and local students.

Students learn to respect and protect animal life found in local habitats like this marshy meadow.

wanted to make sure that every little kid was involved, so even the kindergarten kids planted a tree. The students worked in teams to plant the large trees, smaller trees and shrubs."

A year later, the preparations for Phase Two began with a dramatic transformation in the school landscape. When the Terraview-Willowfield school population returned for the first day of school in 1999, a remarkable sight greeted them: the field facing their school was no longer there. Instead, there was a new, gently sloping landscape that led down to the irregularly curving shores of a freshly dug pond, complete with an island in the middle. The stretch of Taylor/Massey Creek adjoining the school now emptied into the new pond. City Parks staff arrived soon after with bulldozers to plant some large trees on the pond's shores. And then the community — including Terraview-Willowfield students, staff and parents — went to work.

"The shrubs were selected because they were part of the natural environment and would survive," explained Sheriff-Scott. "The plants were also selected to help make the area safe for the children as well as to regenerate the natural environment," she added. "For example, bulrushes grow quickly and become very dense, preventing the children from seeing the water line. The new shrubs protect them by providing a visible barrier."

The school organized a planting day, and once again community members joined participants from the school. Together, they planted small trees such as cedars, Canadian hemlock and willows to frame the pond's edge. They planted shrubs — including red osier dogwood, raspberry, service-berry, nannyberry, high bush cranberry and riverbank grape — to naturalize the newly graded shores. For colour and beauty, they planted flowering plants, smooth wild roses, gold drop cinquefoil and day lilies.

Families of mallard ducks and Canada geese have been quick to spot this new, sheltered aquatic paradise. And, to the great excitement of the students, a great blue heron has been sighted several times. As they watch their regenerated creek valley become a healthy natural space, the students are learning to do simple water quality assessment. Alison Luck's Grade 8 students have collected samples to assist the Toronto Region Conservation Authority (TRCA) with their water monitoring. They have also begun to look at and compare the differences in water quality in the Phase One (upstream) and the Phase Two (downstream) sections of their project.

The transformed school grounds offer learning opportunities for every grade. Adrian Rizza found that the naturalized space across from the school provides a wealth of ideas for teaching his Grade 6 students. Classroom study with field guides in advance of learning outdoors produced vivid results: "When we went outside, students had to list the trees that they had identified. They had to sketch the different foliage and plants that they didn't recognize. After it was all over, we sat in a circle and everyone compared diagrams, and the groups did presentations. It was fabulous! Kids don't realize that when you talk about ecosystems, there are ecosystems right in their own backyard!"

TERRAVIEW–WILLOWFIELD P.S.
An ambitious Don River watershed restoration project transformed a grassy field into a glimmering pond and nature resource for this fortunate school.

HUMBERWOOD DOWNS ACADEMY

Connecting to the Water

Humberwood Downs Academy was built in the mid-1990s on a small piece of property that borders a provincially designated Environmentally Sensitive Area (ESA) in the Humber River Valley. This unusual proximity of the site to a large natural area led the former Etobicoke Board of Education, together with its partners, the Toronto Catholic School Board and the then City of Etobicoke, to make a special effort to harmonize the building with its natural environment. Humberwood Downs Academy is a unique school in the ways that it demonstrates care of the environment through its design. No less important than care in the building design has been the care in staffing. Science teacher and outdoor educator Lynn Short was hired specifically to fulfill the mandate of providing environmental programs for all primary and junior classes. Principal Greg Freeman has played a key role by setting timetables that make Short available to classes during each teacher's preparation time. His leadership and support have been crucial to the success of these unique environmental programs.

Short is a medical researcher turned teacher and a part-time conservation area employee. A dynamo of environmental expertise, activity, enthusiasm and inspiration, she is passionate about the outdoors and has shaped her career to transmit that love to students. "I love being outdoors, and so I want to share that with the kids. I think that's really, really important. Even if you can reach half of them, hopefully they'll develop a caring attitude towards what's going on around them, so that it doesn't disappear before they grow up."

Short describes the naturalization projects at Humberwood Downs by beginning with the water. An important consideration in the school's planning process was ecologically sound management of the water running off the school site to avoid losing it into the sewer system. "All of the water

that falls on this site — in order to have the school here — must be rerouted back into the river. So all the water that falls on the roof is redirected into a habitat corridor that goes around the school, under a couple of bridges and eventually back into a creek that flows into the Humber River." Using contemporary techniques in environment-friendly construction, the school has built a small pond on its property as part of its water-management and filtration scheme and as a site for habitat rehabilitation. The pond plays the special role of a wetland in filtering water on its way back into the protected area. Over its six years, the pond at Humberwood Downs has come to blend in with the natural surroundings. Short explained, "When we built it, there was very little vegetation; most of it came in from the meadows — cattails, tall grasses, loosestrife (I'll talk about that later); now it's almost completely covered in cattails, as we'd anticipated. We keep hoping for the day when a muskrat moves in; that's happened at the Humber College pond."

HUMBERWOOD DOWNS ACADEMY
Rainwater is filtered and re-routed to replenish ground water and the neighbouring Humber River, rather than lost to the sewer system.

HILLSIDE OUTDOOR EDUCATION SCHOOL
Nature's abundance in a school naturalization project.

The special appeal of learning at Humberwood Downs lies in the endless opportunities for discovery in the natural beauty of the valley in which it lies. In order to blend in with the surrounding conservation land, the school's landscaping reflects the respect for nature shown by its neighbours. When the school building was first erected, the contractors provided it with a surrounding habitat corridor to offer a mix of cover for birds and small animals, and an ornamental landscape for humans. "We've got forsythia in there, a lot of red osier dogwood and plants that would provide some food for the birds," Short said. "This is a migration route, this river valley, so we do get migrating species." Nature has been allowed to reclaim the marshy meadow beside the school — up to a point. "That area has been allowed to naturalize," continued Short. "We don't make any attempt to weed it. We keep it trimmed so that it's not too high, for safety. But we do allow any species that takes root to grow there." And for student naturalists and community members who enjoy

nature walks, grassy walkways allow safe and easy access to the naturalized spaces.

The Humber Arboretum, a neighbouring institution and invaluable resource that shares the valley, has taken on the role of horticultural consultant for Humberwood Downs Academy. Arboretum staff have contributed their expertise in suggesting sites and species for plantings as the school has acquired funding for naturalization projects.

The work at Humberwood Downs reflects a growing awareness of and sensitivity to the important functions of wetlands in southern Ontario's landscape. Over the last two hundred years, more than 70 percent of its wetlands have been drained to make way for homes and farms. The school offers an excellent example of how building design can contribute to the health of ecosystems.

HUMBERWOOD DOWNS ACADEMY'S LOOSESTRIFE STORY

The Humberwood Downs community has come in direct contact with one of Ontario's most beautiful and invasive alien species: purple loosestrife has taken hold in the valley. Lynn Short told the story of the school's joint experiment with the Humber Arboretum in integrated pest management, using a natural insect "enemy" to control the loosestrife, rather than poisonous herbicides to eliminate it.

"The big problem was that the loosestrife was here, but none of its predators were. And it's such a prolific seeder: it grows from cuttings, and there's really nothing you can do to stop it. Guelph University had a research team that was looking into the beetles that the loosestrife is a specific host for. They're European beetles; they're a non-native species; they feed on loosestrife specifically. It's a method that's been used with some success around Ontario, although it's never going to eradicate it. About three years ago we obtained some of the

beetles from Guelph University, and we released them here in the meadow. The first year we looked for them and we didn't see anything. And the second year, we didn't see anything. The loosestrife had kept growing; I guessed the beetles hadn't worked. Well, this year, the superintendent of the Humber Arboretum and I both, almost simultaneously on his side and on my side of the meadow, found them — the beetles were there and the larvae were there, and there were holes in the loosestrife. They must have reached a critical mass so now you can actually see them. So we're really hopeful next year that things will get even more exciting!"

Short made the invasive loosestrife and the integrated pest management a subject of discussion and exploration with her students. She asked them to do a survey to see how many beetles and larvae they could find around their pond. "Every class that went out talked about it. When they were first looking," she recalled, "they saw the beetles. And then the beetles disappeared. But they had to look *under* the leaves, because the larvae feed on the underside. So then they found these little orange larvae, caterpillars without fur. So they actually were in the meadow. The beetles didn't make a huge dent, but we're really hopeful that next year, the loosestrife will be under control. It was pretty exciting."

Lynn Short has made it her life's work to connect young children with the outdoors through meaningful hands-on experience. "One of the first things I do with the kids when we come out of the school is we all take a deep breath: 'Doesn't it smell better out here than it does in there? It's not stuffy. It's clean air. It's fresh. Isn't this better to be out here? Walls all stay the same. Floors stay the same. And desks all stay the same. But the places where we learn change.' I want them to feel that, and grow with it."

BROADACRES PUBLIC SCHOOL

Rehabilitating a Swale

At Broadacres Public School in Etobicoke, the Naturalization Committee, in partnership with the local Parks and Forestry Department, adopted a piece of grass-covered parkland adjoining the school property and carried out a habitat rehabilitation project on this open space. A feature of their chosen site was a depression, or a swale, which captures rainwater runoff in wet weather and channels it into a storm sewer. The naturalization of the swale became one of Broadacres's three large-scale gardening projects, in addition to a courtyard garden (described in chapter 3) and a playground field garden (described in chapter 4).

Naturalization projects at Broadacres are planned through the co-operative efforts of the Naturalization Committee, composed of teachers and parents, and the student Green Team. Green Team members give advice to the Naturalization Committee and take information from its members back to the classroom for feedback from other students. The adults feel it is important that the students have input so that they develop a strong sense of ownership and responsibility for gardening projects. The Naturalization Committee prides itself

BROADACRES P.S.
A long-horned grasshopper, one of Ontario's katydids that "sings" by rubbing its wings together.

on the mix of age and experience of its members, the regular attendance of the vice-principal and eight of the school's staff of twenty teachers, and the principal's ongoing support. It has also had significant participation from the parent community, including an outstanding contribution of time and expertise from Debby Morton, who played a key role in planning, acting as liaison and fundraising.

Kathy Caulfield, a teacher and the chair of the Naturalization Committee, described how the swale project was organized. Prior to planting, committee members conducted site visits with Parks and Forestry Department staff, who agreed to create a no-cut zone in the area to be naturalized. (It should be noted that partnerships between the Parks and Forestry Department and citizens' groups or schools are proving to be mutually beneficial, as mowing schedules in some jurisdictions are being curtailed and interest in low-maintenance, naturalized spaces increases.) Morton described the partnership with the department's staff members as friendly, helpful and encouraging. "They even supported us in our attempt to grow wetland plants despite being somewhat pessimistic about our chances of success," she added.

The swale was planted over a period of a month, late in May and early in June. Classes were scheduled to go out every day, with the students co-operating in the various tasks of digging, laying out circles to plant in, and mulching. Another part of the swale rehabilitation project involved building a small retention pond to trap runoff water that flowed through the swale itself, which in turn would create a wetland. By placing some of the sod removed from a proposed water retention site downstream towards the drain, the students, under the supervision of their teachers, constructed a small dam. Cattails and swamp milkweed were planted in this newly created wetland area to see if they would survive a variety of moisture conditions over different seasons.

Applewood House, a neighbourhood historical site, allowed the Naturalization Committee to use its water supply after the planting, a generous and essential support in caring for a newly planted area which the school water supply could not reach. This successful co-operative organizing, and the rallying of the entire Broadacres school population to carry out the swale's naturalization, was a cause for celebration. "When we finished, we had a 'swaleabration,' with a hotdog lunch for everyone!" beamed Caulfield. "We worked very hard, and we did it!"

Seven years later, the swale has the air of a mature meadow. The cattails and the swamp milkweed have demonstrated their ability to thrive (despite the cautions of the Parks and Forestry staff) through both wet and dry conditions, possibly as a result of their low-lying proximity to the local water table. As well, natural processes are reclaiming this former grass-covered parkland. In some places, thistles have come and gone and have been replaced by the next phase of perennial goldenrods. A few "invasives" have arrived and stayed, including Manitoba maples, Norway maples and Canada thistle. For the Naturalization Committee, some challenges remain — for example, finding the best methods to control "invasives" and making a long-term maintenance plan.

A fox has come to live on the swale, and ground-nesting killdeer fly above it. Cardinals nest in the evergreens, and mallard ducks arrive to visit the wetland in the early spring. The Broadacres community has brought a successional meadow into being, and will derive satisfaction from the success of rehabilitating this natural area and benefit from a wealth of future learning opportunities through observing the swale's growth and change over time.

EASTDALE COLLEGIATE INSTITUTE

Creating an Urban Woodland

When teacher Neil Langley arrived at Eastdale Collegiate Institute in the fall of 1997, he looked out the window of one of his new classrooms onto an abandoned daycare play-space full of patchy grass. In his mind's eye, he imagined a garden, so he asked some of his students how they would feel about creating a woodland area beside the school building. "It sounded pretty interesting," recalled Grade 12 student Aaron Shaw, who was then a new Grade 9 student at Eastdale. "I'd planted trees before, but I'd never been involved in a project like this."

Aaron and some classmates organized a garden group that met once a week. They set out to learn about native woodland plant species and discussed potential designs for the space. They also made some inquiries about funding sources. The students' initial funding proposal, to the Toronto Optimist Club, netted them their first thousand dollars. The following spring, garden group members attended the Board's annual Student Environment Network conference, and chose workshops on school-ground transformation through gardening, and on resources available to support gardening projects.

JOHN G. ALTHOUSE MIDDLE SCHOOL
Native species populate this urban woodland.

The Eastdale gardeners took the first step in preparing their chosen site by attempting to smother the remaining grass with plastic laid down over the winter. When the winds blew the covering away, the students found themselves faced with the spring task of pulling up the grass, and under that a confusion of roots, by hand. Once exposed, the soil proved to be poor and filled with bricks and stones left over from construction, a problem they remedied by ordering a truckload of new topsoil through the Board's grounds department.

Aaron and the garden group drew up their own design for Eastdale's Native Woodland Garden in consultation with horticulturalist Dagmar Baur, who suggested plant species

LOW-MAINTENANCE GARDENING

Habitat rehabilitation projects have a lesser need for continual maintenance than discrete gardens. In their early stages, new plants require watering, mulching and weeding, but once established, areas that are naturalized can remain healthy with less frequent human contact. This is an important consideration for gardening groups that may not have the where-withal to provide the more highly organized and time-demanding care that discrete gardens need. Regenerating areas need to be kept litter-free, trimmed along their borders to keep them attractive, checked and weeded for potentially invasive species, and have larger plants and trees pruned to avoid overcrowding. They may also have new plant material added to them to enhance natural succession processes. But for schools where continuity may be an issue in recruiting help for garden maintenance, habitat rehabilitation projects can offer both an environmental and an educational return as well as the benefits of fewer maintenance hours. In rehabilitation projects, nature takes over where human efforts began.

that would suit the site conditions. Over the course of three planting days, the students translated their plan on paper into an actual landscape, adjusting their design to the requirements of the plants. Plant choices for their woodland garden included a mix of native shrubs and grasses, ferns, flowering understorey plants and vines. Their experiment was to see if eventually this reintroduced community of native plants and grasses could become self-maintaining in the urban core.

Aaron Shaw is optimistic about Eastdale's habitat rehabilitation effort becoming a contribution to long-term change. "I see the garden as building something, starting something new, planting history," he reflected. "Twenty years down the line when I'm driving my solar-powered car down the street with my kids, I'll say, 'I went to this high school, I put those rocks there, I planted those trees,' and they'll say, 'That's impossible, Dad! Look how big they are!'"

RUNNYMEDE PUBLIC SCHOOL

A Nature Garden

At Runnymede Public School, the school community has seen the slope behind and beside the building transformed over ten years from a traditional green lawn to a shady native garden. As in many other successful naturalization projects, Runnymede's group wisdom held that the project should begin on a small scale and grow with the knowledge acquired by the gardeners.

The first phase of Runnymede's garden was a joint project conceived by parent Karen Yukich and then-student-teacher Karyn Morris, who had a passionate interest in gardens. They invited Morris's Grades 4 and 5 students to design their own garden, for which Runnymede's parent Environment Committee would then secure funding and organize the actual planting. Karyn Morris took her class on

RUNNYMEDE P.S.

In the shade of a reforested slope, students record their observations in their own nature study area.

**A *harvest*
of organic
tomatoes.**

a field trip to neighbouring High Park to introduce the students to local plant communities; the garden project became the focus of curriculum planning for that term.

"In that first year we worked from the kids' plans, which were based on a Ministry of Natural Resources book called *Landscaping for Wildlife*," recounted Yukich. "It wasn't really based on an ecosystem approach; it was more like, 'Here are some bushes that give berries for birds, and here are some trees that give berries for birds.'" Morris' students were divided into twelve groups, each with the task of designing a garden plot. Each plot was to include three trees and some undergrowth, with the students selecting plant species from different categories to include in their designs. The overall plan for this first phase was set up so that the students' small plots, planted together, would constitute one harmonious whole.

As they worked through that first year, the Runnymede group began to see the naturalization process differently. "The second year we developed a whole master plan," continued Yukich. "As a parent group, we tried to do more of an overall ecosystem approach." One parent member of the Environment Committee made a detailed life study to assess the growing conditions in different parts of their site. Based on her report, the committee divided the available growing space into different types of small plant community zones. Looking at a sketch of the evolving planting plan, Yukich described the plant communities they chose to represent. "You can see we had a prairie area

Learning Native Plants in Hillside's Sample Life-Zone Gardens

The Hillside Outdoor Education School's sample life-zone gardens show examples of Ontario's biodiversity and offer students an introduction to the names of some typical native species.

The Carolinian Canada Life Zone
(which includes Toronto):
black walnut, butternut, bitternut hickory, black maple, tulip tree, sycamore, shagbark hickory, swamp white oak, blue beech, witch hazel, flowering dogwood, ninebark and American hazelnut.

The Great Lakes–St. Lawrence Mixed-Forest Life Zone:
sugar maple, beech, eastern hemlock, eastern white pine, eastern white cedar, white ash, green ash, ironwood, red oak, white oak, burr oak, white elm, black cherry, silver maple, alternate dogwood, red osier dogwood, grey dogwood, nannyberry, serviceberry, staghorn sumach, choke cherry, hawthorne, Witch hazel, wild currant, and gooseberry.

The Boreal Forest Life Zone:
black spruce, white spruce, white birch, trembling aspen, balsam fir, tamarack, green alder, serviceberry, blueberry, bracken fern, wild rose and bush honeysuckle.

here, with the buffalo berries, which was meant to be more open, and we got into some more woodland plantings with maple trees further along, and our white pine grove, which was planted with these little baby white pines, of which there are a few left. We just basically tried to work more on a zone approach: you can see the lower slopes are massive bushes and more like an edge of a forest." In the space of only one year, the project had moved from berry-bearing plants for birds to a far more sophisticated plant-community zone approach.

During the second year, the Runnymede gardeners expanded their plantings in what Yukich described as "skeleton fashion," leaving empty spaces so that over the following few years the new areas could continue to be filled in with compatible zone species. The third year, the gardeners opened up a sodded area and added a new zone of wildflowers and grasses. This section pioneered a new type of planting, "inoculating" the area in the hope that over time the plant material would spread. After this initial period of intense gardening activity at the school in the early 1990s, participation waned and the naturalized area was left to grow more or less on its own. And then, in 1998, a new group of parents became actively involved with the garden.

Runnymede's thriving patch of urban nature is a good example of a habitat rehabilitation project where natural processes have gradually been allowed to prevail. "It was never meant to be a highly managed garden," remarked Yukich. "It's not a no-maintenance garden; it's a *low*-maintenance garden. Recently a small patch of dog-strangling vine (swallowwort) has grown there, which is really a terrible thing to get into the naturalized space, so that's something we need to try to get rid of." Maintenance of Runnymede's naturalized space has become a priority for the second-generation garden group.

In between biannual planting and clean-up days, Ann Lakoff's students participate in periodic cleanups of the

garden site, outfitted with gloves provided by school caretakers and with parental permission to participate. "In half an hour, with the whole class doing it — even less — they can get that whole area cleaned up," she said. The students also learn to help with weeding out undesirable invasive species. "There are tons of sprouting baby trees out there that are not wanted. And it's a constant effort to keep them under control!"

All this involvement and hard work is a very positive experience for Runnymede students. Lakoff feels a strong emotional tie to her school's green space, which she believes is reflected in the enthusiasm the garden inspires. "The way I see kids use the space in the garden, I think that they love it. I've got some really rough-and-tumble guys in the class, and they have been to every single cleanup day we've had for the past three or four years. They have their tree that's got their name on it, and they love that tree, and they take care of it. And they love the digging; they love the physical nature of that whole thing. Kids are enjoying the space, and I'm enjoying the fact that they are."

RANCHDALE PUBLIC SCHOOL
Growing Trees from Seed

By its second year of existence under the direction of Grade 2 teacher David Barnes, the Ranchdale Public School Naturalization Club had ninety members. Barnes and the club members have already planted vegetable and butterfly gardens. In addition, with funding assistance from the Toronto Atmospheric Fund and from LEAF (Local Enhancement and Appreciation of Forests), they have planted nearly fifty good-sized "anchor" trees in the meadow on their school property in North York. From that solid start, and with the determination to continue expanding their habitat rehabilitation area without spending any more

money, they set financial independence as their next goal. "We've decided to grow our own trees," declared Barnes.

"Last year we experimented and planted birch seeds in pots indoors," he explained. "We grew them in greenhouse trays in the windows, replanted them into pots and then around June transplanted them outside to the vegetable garden, where they're protected, to mature. Finally we transplanted them in the meadow area we're trying to reforest. They're now about a third of a metre tall, maybe because we head-started them in January. So now we know we can grow birch trees."

Encouraged by their success with birch seedlings, the young Ranchdale foresters decided to expand their efforts. "We dug out large oval patches — maybe two-by-two metres — of lawn," Barnes continued. "It really wasn't that much effort to take out the grass; the kids enjoyed that. We mulched up the soil, worked in wood chips and planted birch seeds and acorns and maple keys. They're randomly placed at the bottom of our hill, in the tall grass area. We hope that in the spring we'll start to see them sprouting. It will be interesting to see what comes up."

Naturalization Club members have also put some of their acorn collection to overwinter in cold storage. "We'll start them in the spring in the classroom, while we have some others starting outside naturally," said Barnes, "so there's a sort of double insurance that we'll have trees to plant."

David Barnes believes that this approach helps young students realize that efforts to restore nature take patience. "Growing trees from seed is a great way to naturalize. It takes a long time to get the trees to any size, but the kids learn that you can't recreate a natural area by just taking a few trees and plopping them in the ground. Nature takes time and many years to get to what it used to be. That's a very important lesson. We think we can just replace things quickly, but in fact it takes hundreds of years of growth. And eventually we'll teach them, too, that once we have a bit of a forest there we'll monitor it and see how it develops. If we want to recreate habitat for migratory species and create species for some resident species, then we're going to have to find ways to naturalize that don't cost a lot of money, because there isn't necessarily a lot of money out there. And once we have more habitat, we want to put up bird feeders and birdhouses that the kids can build in the nature club or classes."

David Barnes sees naturalization as a school activity that offers enormous learning potential. "Everywhere we look there's another part of a lesson plan out there. Every time you take the kids out there they learn so much — and they enjoy their learning." But the students also find the naturalized areas a good place to play. "The kids love it — they're out catching grasshoppers that weren't there before. When I first read about nature projects, I read there was a decrease in schoolyard arguments, pushing, shoving, and now I see so many kids out discovering things instead of pushing and shoving one another. They're looking at nature. It's so exciting for them."

*

RUNNYMEDE P.S.
"Kids love the space in the garden, ... the physical nature ot it."
— teacher Ann Lakoff

Some of Toronto's outdoor education schools have also started engaging students in naturalization and habitat rehabilitation projects as part of their programs. Two of Toronto's outdoor education schools are located in natural areas within the city limits and their staff have recognized the value of habitat rehabilitation as a teaching tool.

HILLSIDE OUTDOOR EDUCATION SCHOOL

Hillside Outdoor Education School is strategically situated between part of Toronto's eastern suburbs and the country's second largest urban park, Rouge Park. The fenceline that separates the school's lawn from the forest and the valley beyond was chosen as a place where school staff and conservationists could work together to create three sample plant communities. There, plant groupings from three of Ontario's four life zones — the Carolinian, the Great Lakes — St. Lawrence and the Boreal — were planted to help students learn to identify the species and patterns of nature they'll find in wild places.

Hillside's three life-zone teaching gardens, which will be allowed to run wild along the fenceline (requiring only low maintenance to keep invasive species out), offer a first stop for students on their way to the adjoining Rouge Valley, where they observe nature or help with restorative plantings. Individual characteristic plant species are labelled to familiarize students with their names. One of Hillside's goals is to help visiting students learn to identify five different trees, five different plants and five different amphibians.

FOREST VALLEY OUTDOOR EDUCATION SCHOOL

Forest Valley Outdoor Education School in North York — a site that for many years had been used as a summer camp with open expanses of swimming pools, basketball courts, minigolf and playing fields — became a large-scale habitat rehabilitation project in 1993. In that year, the summer camp use of the site was discontinued, and this became an opportunity for the staff to plan a totally new landscape for this secluded piece of the Don River Valley. "We wanted to give the land back to the land," said site manager and outdoor educator Sandee Sharpe of the early planning phase. "We cautiously planned a green, natural outdoor learning environment to mirror the surrounding forest."

When the old outbuildings and sports facilities were demolished, the land was regraded and the newly barren parts of the ground seeded with a varied grass-seed mix to stabilize the earth with what they call "mother plants." The renaturalized space was declared an Environmentally Sensitive Area (ESA), and an "elephant steps" path made of logs was installed so that students could walk through the regenerating area without trampling it. Over the following seven years, Forest Valley's land became a fitting reflection of its name.

The Forest Valley staff recognized that students couldn't become ecologically literate in one or two visits to their outdoor school. In 1997, to mark thirty years of outdoor education in North York, they celebrated by initiating their Board-wide naturalization project. "What we were looking for was a much deeper, longer-lasting connection," declared Sharpe. Forest Valley invited local educators to join site staff in developing naturalization activities that could be carried out on school grounds. "We know that teachers have a list of things that they need to do. We don't want to give them one other thing; we want to show them that this can make their lives easier," Sharpe observed. They settled on ecological monitoring as a beneficial activity and developed two ecological monitoring areas. One was a Go Wild area that allows students to observe what happens to a disturbed site when nature is free to follow its own course. The second site lets students observe changes in plant succession. It contains ten spaces within a ten-by-twenty-metre plot of ground. Each year, an additional two-metre strip is left to grow wild to demonstrate the first three years and successive periods of growth and change in plant diversity. Forest Valley staff keep photographic records of evolving naturalized areas to help students understand the changes that occur over time.

Ecological monitoring areas require no planting. The learning is in observing and recording nature's changes. "The variety of plants observed in the first and second year totally changes," noted Sharpe. "There's one that immediately comes to mind: the predominance of goldenrod. It emits a chemical in the soil that discourages other plant growth. It's not surprising that that area is taken over by goldenrod, but it's wonderful just to see how it's changing." Many students experience the monitoring exercise as an introduction to plant life, ecology, diversity of species, or "how everything is interconnected," as Sharpe remarked. "There's probably no area in the curriculum that isn't covered by that."

FOREST VALLEY OUTDOOR EDUCATION SCHOOL
A serene reforested outdoor learning environment.

chapter 6 # A CANOPY OF GREEN
THE SPECIAL ROLE OF TREES

To plant trees is to give body and life to one's dreams
of a better world.

— RUSSELL PAGE,
THE EDUCATION OF A GARDENER

WALKING UNDER TREES on a warm day in cooling shade and
dappled sunlight offers a very tangible sensation of how trees
influence both the beauty and the comfort of a place. Their
presence significantly changes the character of a landscape.
In Toronto, trees are one of the outstanding visual elements
of our urban environment and define our sense of place. The
city is exceptional in the quality of its "urban forest." In the
summer months, a view from the top of the CN Tower
reveals vast sweeps of green across the city's neighbourhoods,
parks, ravines and schoolyards, where a variety of mature
trees — the envy of other large North American cities —
provide shade and beauty. On school grounds, as on the
grounds of other public institutions, trees are a traditional
and important element of the landscape.

THE FORESTS AND THE TREES

Thinking ecologically, it is always wise to consider any particular kind of vegetation within an expanded geographic
context. Before looking at trees in our schoolyards, it is
important to look first beyond the limits of Toronto and
survey the wider ecosystem of southern Ontario, now and
historically.

When European settlement began in Ontario in the late
1700s, more than 90 percent of the land was covered with
densely wooded old-growth Carolinian forest. The early
settlers cleared and burned vast areas, and the mighty native
pines and oaks, legendary for their size and quality, found
ready markets both locally and abroad. Heavy harvesting of
southern Ontario's woodlands continued throughout the
1990s, even in conservation areas. Today, 80 percent of the
woodlands south and east of the Canadian Shield are gone,
removed to make room for farmland, urban development
and, more recently, suburban sprawl. Less than 6 percent of
the south is still original woodland, and only .07 percent of
southern Ontario's land base can claim forest stands that are
more than 120 years old. Most of the remaining woodlands
are fragmented, with many covering less than three hectares.
These ecological islands are for the most part too young and
small to allow for the optimal functioning of complex
ecosystems. Small remnant habitats and isolated species
populations are vulnerable to extinction: since 1961, southern Ontario's interior forests' songbird populations —
including species such as scarlet tanagers, wood thrushes,
ovenbirds and veeries — have declined by more than 50 percent. Forest-core habitat (or deep forest, which is defined as
more than 100 metres from the nearest edge) exists in only a
few of southern Ontario's remaining woodlots.[9]

As more people have become aware of the importance of
preserving woodland biodiversity, however, the southern
Ontario forest cover has made something of a comeback in
recent years, particularly on the Niagara Escarpment and in
many of our watersheds. People are making efforts to
determine the significance of existing woodlands and

proposing evaluation criteria for land-use planning decisions. Many are attempting to preserve the integrity of natural ecosystems and communities of native plants and to protect rare and endangered species. In partnership with educational programs, landowners have contributed to local watershed protection through the maintenance or restoration of riverbank vegetation on their properties. Some conservation groups are working to connect existing remnant forests with corridor plantings that allow for the sheltering and movement of wildlife. This range of strategies for restoration and conservation offers the hope that ecosystem protection and the maintenance of species diversity will eventually become an integral part of development in southern Ontario.

NATURE AND NATURAL PROCESSES IN THE CITY

But what does all this have to do with trees in schoolyards? Nature is not only found in the country. It is also found around us in the city, and we are intimately connected to it. The evolving discipline of urban ecology suggests that as world population continues to grow — and with nearly half of the global population now residing in urban environments — cities have a vital role to play in the nurturing of local biodiversity and the health of natural systems that support healthy human populations. When parks, ravines and private yards are included, Toronto's urban forest spreads across 20 percent of the city's area. This forest has a very different kind of diversity from the outlying Carolinian ecosystem, but it can offer a completely new dimension when the trees and other species present are considered as a system rather than as a random collection of landscaping elements. When seen as contributing to beautifying the city as well as providing a remarkable set of ecological services, trees take on added value and importance.

Trees provide summer shade, buffer cold winter winds and reduce energy costs; they boost property values, reduce water runoff and soil erosion, filter dust, block noise and provide habitat and shelter for songbirds and other urban wildlife. In addition, they renew our oxygen and add moisture to the air through transpiration. Within our depleted ozone layer, they block close to 60 percent of the sun's rays. Trees also filter air pollution, taking in such noxious gases as sulphur dioxide, nitrogen dioxide, ground-level ozone, carbon monoxide and microscopic particles that contribute to smog.

Trees also absorb carbon dioxide, a principal greenhouse gas that contributes to climate change. A landmark study done in Chicago in 1994 revealed that larger city trees were

Holding down soil, shading the earth and cooling its surface, absorbing rainwater and gradually re-releasing moisture, softening the sweep of winds, trees are a major climate regulator in our country and on our planet ... The importance of maintaining our green canopy cannot be overemphasized. Climate moderation is perhaps the most essential — and the least recognized — role of our trees.

HENRY KOCK, INTERPRETIVE
HORTICULTURALIST, GUELPH ARBORETUM

HILLSIDE OUTDOOR EDUCATION SCHOOL

Nature's artistry in the Rouge Valley.

end of their days and being replaced by smaller species with shorter life expectancies. This is a result of such factors as increased urban density, growing demand for parking in front of homes and the removal of topsoil by developers in newly built areas. Losing old trees is a problem because their disappearance means the loss of valuable natural processes: new trees require many years to re-establish the desirable shady ambience of their predecessors and to reach a size that lets them work best to improve the quality of city air. Landscape architect and urban ecologist Michael Hough refers to such plantings as "a landscape without a future."[11] Unlike natural forests, urban forests are not self-renewing. In other words, if younger trees are not strategically introduced to create a more natural distribution of age, our children may not enjoy the same quality of a mature urban-forest canopy that we do now.

TREES AT SCHOOL

Tree plantings on school properties have, for the most part, followed the traditional landscape patterns adopted by municipal parks departments. Individual — and sometimes exotic ornamental — trees tend to be spaced out, "lollipop style," across expanses of lawn to provide shady areas at the front of school property without reducing the amount of ground space available for human use. Playground areas have typically been left bare of vegetation to keep outdoor space free for play. But with the growing awareness of the many compelling reasons for greening urban and suburban school grounds, tree planting has provided the means to produce one of the simplest, and at the same time one of the most rewarding, changes that can be made to school property.

When choosing a type of tree to add to a school ground, it is important to look not only at the specific space where a new tree might be planted but also at the wider environs of

able to absorb up to ninety times more carbon dioxide than those with smaller trunk diameters and canopies.[10] The Chicago study concluded that it would require nine million dollars worth of pollution control equipment to match the work of the city's urban forest in purifying the air! The results of this report so impressed the City of Toronto that it has commissioned a similar study.

Our city trees, it is clear, are enormously valuable assets in improving the quality of our lives. But the composition of the city's mature urban forest is gradually changing. Staff at Toronto's Parks and Forestry Department report that the stately old trees in the city's oldest neighbourhoods, many planted over a hundred years ago, are gradually reaching the

the school. A little research into the history of the local ecology can offer some insights as to the type of ecosystem that once flourished there. Place names are sometimes indicative of former and present ecological features: Oakwood Collegiate Institute in central Toronto, for instance, is named after an estate that once occupied part of an oak savannah. The neighbourhood surrounding the school still has many beautiful old oaks along its streets and in private yards. To maintain the health of the oak population in that part of the city, therefore, it would be beneficial to plant new oak trees to ensure a succession of these mighty shade trees.

Trees, then, are an essential part of the community — part of its cooling system, part of the maintenance of climate-moderating, part of its history and its beauty. So what is the best way to plant and nurture a new generation of trees? Horticulturalist Henry Kock is an educator teaching schools and communities the best ways of restoring local ecosystems. His first piece of advice to would-be propagators of healthy native trees is to look for long-lived trees. "You need to go to the oldest surviving trees in our city," Kock recommends, "because they have withstood the test of time." Their immune systems have persevered in warding off diseases, and they have tolerated extreme climate and air pollution conditions. To Kock, they're triple survivors, and their seeds should be selected for the regeneration of their species.

Next, he advises, trees should be selected by their place, not by those who are planting them. "We have to stop choosing the tree. Humans must not choose the tree; the site has to choose the tree. And it is important to choose what has proven to be a sturdy tree. You'll see this in your local neighbourhood through the big old trees that are still there: silver maple, oak, American elm." The third important piece of advice is to create and maintain a canopy of green by adding new trees over time. "When you go into a natural woodland, you see unevenly aged mixed species," observes Kock. "And this is what you can do on school property. That's why the

worst thing to do in a schoolyard naturalization project is to install it all at once. It has to be extended over the maximum amount of time —twenty years — so that every four years a new part of the project is completed. And we have to stop thinking about how many trees we're planting and think about the *quality* of trees we're putting into the ground, and about seed source, placement and appropriate site-species match, which takes good science. It's an important lesson in problem-solving, and there's all kinds of room in the curriculum for that."

Trees are an investment in the future. Schools that plant new trees are engaging in an act of giving to succeeding generations. Site manager Sandee Sharpe of the Forest Valley Outdoor School shares this piece of wisdom with her students: "Everybody should plant a tree that they will never sit under! It will just be there for somebody else."

chapter 7 RECONNECTING CHILDREN TO NATURE

SCHOOL GARDENS IN THE TWENTY-FIRST CENTURY

A revolution in education is underway and it is starting in the most unlikely places. The revolutionaries are not professional educators from famous universities: rather, they are elementary school students, a growing number of intrepid teachers, and a handful of facilitators from widely diverse backgrounds. The goal of the revolution is the reconnection of young people to their own habitats and communities. The classroom is the ecology of the surrounding community, not the confining four walls of the traditional school. And the pedagogy of the revolution is simply a process of organizing engagement with living systems and the lives of people who live by the grace of those systems.

— DAVID ORR,
ECOLITERACY: MAPPING THE TERRAIN

AFTER A LONG HISTORY of offering children valuable lessons in many things — Botany, Geography, Mathematics, beautification, civic pride, the dignity of labour and the growing of food — the school gardening movement is ready to take students into the twenty-first century. Over the past decade, the outdoor classrooms and naturalized areas developed in Europe and North America have uncovered their potential for new learning and for reconnecting children to nature. Since 1991, Evergreen, one of Canada's strongest supporters of school-ground naturalization, has been working "to bring communities and nature together for the benefit of both." The organization's work includes the task of fostering the development of gardens, which Evergreen refers to as learning grounds, by helping individual schools transform parts of their property from barren, asphalt surfaces into dynamic natural outdoor classrooms.

In 2001, Evergreen and the Toronto District School Board formalized a partnership though the joint hiring of a schoolyard greening design facilitator to assist Toronto schools in their gardening efforts. Cam Collyer, national manager of Evergreen's Learning Grounds program, reflected on the work of bringing nature to school children, beginning with taking responsibility for the commons, the public places and natural amenities we all share. "This is a preparation for our young students, an engagement in the commons. School is our first experience of the commons ... for which we need to build stewardship. What excites me the most about our work is seeing people light up at the opportunity of being involved — because all of a sudden there is an opportunity to become engaged in changing this public landscape. They are seeing the results of their own work, their own creativity and their own ability to solve problems."

Engaging in habitat rehabilitation on school grounds is another important contribution that school communities

and programs. A green infrastructure includes space to sustain the biodiversity of native plants and animal communities, as well as creating connections that allow interchange between native plants and animal communities. It also helps to maintain the health of native ecosystems and landscapes by sustaining their physical, chemical and biological processes.

Direct contact with land, water, soil and plants can provide teachers and students with new bridges to real-world issues of food, community, urban planning and design, air and water quality, energy consumption, healthy cities, habitat preservation and biodiversity. The knowledge and learning skills developed in the investigation of these areas can involve students at any grade level. Experiential learning also offers teachers many opportunities to meet formal curriculum requirements in Science, Language, Social Studies, Mathematics, Art, Drama and Music in a number of ways. Such diversity offers young children an enriched context for recognizing the interconnections among different areas of their learning and their own real connections to culture and nature.

Diversity is what horticulturist Henry Kock identifies as a key attribute in the plant world, and not only in the native plant world. While there is considerable (and needed) emphasis on the restoration of plants and habitat native to local places in the school gardening movement, the future also holds a place for a broader understanding of the plants imported into our urban environments. "We're not native to this place," Kock reminds us. "We brought many of these plants with us. We brought our food and our medicine plants with us, and our horticultural plants that are interesting and very beautiful. They are part of our culture. And so I think that a school ground should include a garden that speaks to our ancestral lands as well."

Many of the familiar plants around us carry with them unguessed-at histories, a basis for the study of migrations and transmissions of culture. All the imported plants that

make to the expansion of the green infrastructure within our city. Like schools, professionals are also integrating green elements into urban design. City planners and engineers are joining ranks with nature conservationists to expand the meaning of infrastructure. Our *built infrastructure* includes roads, bridges, electric power lines and water systems, as well as social institutions such as hospitals, libraries and schools. Ecological thinking suggests using the air, land and water to help create a *green infrastructure* that benefits wildlife and people, links urban settings to rural ones and (like built infrastructure) forms an integral part of government budgets surround us can speak, if we listen, of their special qualities and of the ingenuity of the pople who transplanted them. Aboriginal peoples imported and hybridized corn and butternut squash to suit local growing conditions in Ontario. European settlers used garlic mustard as a seasoning and planted hedgerows to provide nuts, berries and windbreaks. Our familiar food staples tomatoes, potatoes, apples and zucchini were also imported.

School gardening invites an investigation of the landscape as an eloquent expression of our multicultural experience. "The options, the diversity of learning opportunities, are missed incredibly if we exclude the non-indigenous plants from our landscape," Kock emphasizes. "They need not be mixed in the same garden. A naturalized landscape is for the indigenous species; another garden is for the introduced plants; and the vegetable garden includes food and medicine plants. And then there are the flowering and fruiting plants, the lilac, the apple. That is what I think is appropriate in a schoolyard. To validate the human experience of moving plants as part of our human reality is important. It's because of that process of over two hundred years of planting non-native plants that we have some of the ecological concerns and difficulties that we perceive now. But the students aren't going to understand that if they don't see both."

GREENING ROOFTOPS

Eastdale Collegiate and Brock Public School

Even in the once-grey world of architecture and engineering, recent innovations are using plants to bridge the traditional divide between the living and non-living environment. Increased interest in an ecological approach to design, urban planning, engineering and architecture has resulted in a recognition of the benefits of harnessing not only the products but also the processes of plants in creating healthy and energy-efficient landscapes, buildings and infrastructures. Some of this new thinking is becoming evident in school gardening projects that offer great promise for the future.

Toronto architect Monica Kuhn is an avid proponent of using rooftop gardening as an integral part of greening the built urban landscape. She described rooftops as "a city's greatest untapped resource, acres of empty space just waiting to be used." Her interest led her to become a founding member of the Rooftop Gardens Resource Group, a volunteer organization that helps design and implement green rooftops. In this capacity, she has lent her assistance and her talents to rooftop-gardening projects in two downtown Toronto schools — one at Eastdale Collegiate Institute and one at Brock Public School. In both cases, students

BROCK P.S.

Plants and sculpture combine to utilize space in this rooftop garden.

participated in the design and development of their rooftop gardens.

In addition to the formal learning opportunities that they share with their earthly counterparts, rooftop gardens have some advantages that are only beginning to be realized. Flat roofs, which are suited to active gardening (as opposed to inaccessible greened roofs, which are becoming popular in Europe as energy-efficient insulation solutions and, more recently, in Tokyo as temperature moderators to counter a serious heat-island effect), are fully open to direct sunlight, and safe from any worry of vandalism. As well, they offer unused space for a garden should ground-level space be limited, and they are excellent laboratories for teaching food production, weather observation and the integration of plants into the urban environment.

Beyond providing another learning ground for students in the school, rooftop gardening also provides secondary benefits to the wider community. Rooftop gardens increase the oxygen output in the city, filter urban air, cut down the "heat island" effect from hard reflective rooftops and capture rainfall, which lessens the burden on the city's storm sewage system. And, according to Kuhn, rooftop gardens can reduce a school's energy consumption by as much as 30 percent, a fact which will appeal to school administrators as energy costs rise. A green roof not only covers and protects the school building, it can also make the roof last longer.

The roof of Eastdale Collegiate Institute, once a 1,830-square-metre sports track, offered a more-than-adequate space to involve students in gardening. "Eastdale has an environmental theme," Kuhn explained. "It's a school for many kids who come back to high school and gardening is related throughout the curriculum to many other subjects." In the mid-1990s, some Danforth Technical School students built cold frames, which they brought to Eastdale's roof to install. The cold frames laid the foundation for a garden composed of raised beds and pots. Funding for further development of

SIR JOHN A. MACDONALD C.I.

Pollination is one of the essential services insects perform to maintain biodiversity in the world.

the school's rooftop garden was provided by the Friends of the Environment of Canada Trust, as well as the local Chinese neighbourhood committee.

"The whole school was involved when the truck brought the soil," recalled student Aaron Shaw of the day they began the rooftop garden. "There's no elevator up to the third floor, so we had enough pails — two hundred! — to bring the soil up. Now we have flowers, vegetables, herbs and papyruses on the roof. The Biology classes use the rooftop garden a lot." Aaron became the summer guardian of the garden during its first two years. "The Science teacher asked me if I would be interested in taking care of her rooftop garden for the summer, and I said yes." Aaron was later to become a driving force behind Eastdale's woodland garden. (See chapter 5.)

At Brock Public School, the impetus behind the rooftop garden project was principal Byron Grant, who contacted Monica Kuhn to ask her advice and guidance. "The school had a group of enthusiastic young teachers," recalled Kuhn, "whom the principal encouraged to take on extracurricular activities. And, as the roof was already used as an outdoor space for staff barbecues and time out, adding a garden improved an already used space."

The students did much of the planning for Brock's rooftop garden. "Everybody can design," observed Kuhn. "This kind of project can help them find out what they know. It demystifies the design process and then teaches them more skills." Each class, kindergarten to Grade 6, made a drawing. "Everyone did amazing plans," she continued, "and the final plan was a combination of them all." Based on the children's sketches, Kuhn and the Rooftop Garden Resource Group finalized the design and layout.

Today, the garden provides planting beds for the different classes, with space for perennials planted by some of the parent volunteers. Under their teachers' guidance, the students choose the plants to be cultivated, with much of the plant material grown in their classrooms in the spring for trans-plantation outside in the warm weather. Other seedlings are grown in the school library, right beside the garden. The older students take on the responsibility of doing the actual planting outdoors when the weather becomes suitable, and the children in Brock's daycare weed and water the garden during the summer.

The focus of Brock's rooftop garden is on food-growing and composting, with learning tied to curriculum wherever possible. Kuhn is pleased by the number of lessons that rooftop gardens can provide: "It begins with aesthetics and design. Teaching kids that they can design lets them claim ownership of space." The students also learn where food comes from and what affects its quality, and they gain a real connection to the cycles of nature, the importance of soil and rain. "Gardens are wonderful demonstration sites for learning about real-world systems," she added. "Gardening is an excellent way to learn about managing waste. In nature *there is no waste*, so students can learn how to reuse materials. They can also learn about unused or wasted space, where things like water and garbage go in urban systems, and what happens there. They can discuss options for alternatives to disposal of various wastes. They can also think about the building — for example, what a roof's made of. They can plant grass on the roof and learn about urban heat islands. All of these concepts can be simplified, even for the younger grades, to help them begin to understand energy savings."

All that said, gardening on the roof of a building does not come without special considerations. Safety, access, liability, weight-bearing structures, roof type and water access are just some of the issues that must be discussed with the Board and the garden designers before initiating any student involvement.

LIVING MACHINES IN THE GREEN INFRASTRUCTURE

In the green infrastructure, mechanical structures and mechanisms can be replaced by systems that use nature's processes to meet human needs. Simple examples are the "living walls" of vegetation at Humberwood Downs Academy and Forest Valley Outdoor Education School (see chapter 3), which, with the same design, have replaced chain-link fence boundaries for child safety and provided habitat for birds. Another simple example is found at Broadacres Public School, where grass-lined drainage ditches or swales keep rainwater runoff in the local water table instead of sending it down the drain into concrete pipes. (See chapter 5.)

A more complex application was installed at the Boyne River Outdoor Education Centre and the Toronto Island School. There, nature's ability to purify water is mimicked in a system called a "living machine," a waste-water treatment centre that cleans water by passing it through a series of tanks located in its greenhouse. The tanks contain organisms ranging from microscopic bacteria and algae to wetland plant communities, as well as (eventually) miniature engineered ecosystems that may include fish and snails. Living machines work by speeding up nature's own water purification processes, using plants and animals — helpful bacteria, plants, snails and fish — that thrive by breaking down and digesting organic pollutants. This type of ecological system treats waste not as waste but as food for other organisms. By using a range of plants, including wetland plants which can remove heavy metal pollutants from water as well as secrete substances that kill pathogens (harmful bacteria), waste water can be returned to a harmless state ready for discharge or recycling back into a building's

ISLAND PUBLIC/NATURAL SCIENCE SCHOOL

The school greenhouse houses a demonstration Living Machine, a biological water-treatment system; solar and photovoltaic panels to make use of "green" energy.

separate non-potable (not for drinking) water system.

This type of waste-water treatment is aesthetic as well as water conserving. A living machine is composed of a series of attractive flower- and plant-filled tanks, waterfalls that flow between them and pools of fish and water plants. In this kind of aquatic greenhouse garden environment, students can learn how to purify waste water by imitating the way natural systems have done it for billions of years.

NEW AWARENESS AND CONNECTIONS THROUGH ENVIRONMENTAL LEARNING

The last two decades of the twentieth century produced the first generation of schools in Toronto dedicated to the rehabilitation of nature. As horticulturalist Henry Kock has reminded many gardeners, "This is the first time in the history of human experience on this earth that we're rebuilding natural landscapes. We've never done this before." And, although school gardening now offers numerous approaches and potentially encompasses a broad range of traditional curriculum content, it has also a deep root in the need to do something about the declining state of the natural world.

What might the role of school gardening be within formal curriculum in helping young people become more

SATEC@W.A. PORTER C.I.

ecologically literate? Many schools undertake naturalization efforts as a means to improve connections between young people and natural environments. Gardening in itself is an expression of valuing contact with nature, and many school gardening projects include specific learning about different aspects of the environment. But a more focused effort at developing ecological literacy in schools is imperative if school staff, parents and local communities wish to see children develop a closer connection to nature which can lead to a better understanding of how to maintain a healthy environment.

Some educators envision making environmental awareness an integral part of formal schooling. The Toronto school system has added an environmental dimension to learning across subject areas. The approach in Toronto uses three ecological organizing concepts: *Sense of Place, Ecosystems Thinking* and *Human Impact.* These were selected to help young people expand the scope of what they learn in school and let them see how many aspects of their learning are interconnected in interesting and practical ways. *Sense of Place* focuses on learning about the world first-hand in a local context. *Ecosystems Thinking* helps develop knowledge of how healthy natural systems, and the way in which people interact with them, provide the basis for sustainable life on earth. *Human Impact* is an invitation to examine the day-to-day choices people make about resource use, food, transportation and lifestyles and a way to evaluate the negative and positive environmental effects of these different choices.

But what, from a formal educational perspective, will be needed in order to make the best pedagogical use of gardens in schools? Our journey through a sampling of Toronto school gardens presents many insights for the future. Perhaps one of the greatest opportunities afforded by learning in gardens is the acquisition of knowledge that keeps students connected to a "bigger picture" as they learn. Learning about

TERRAVIEW–WILLOWFIELD P.S.

Evidence of wildlife returning to naturalized habitats.

the environment is best accomplished and made meaningful through learning in context, learning "by doing" and learning to make wise decisions. New knowledge and skills acquired in a garden can offer students all of these possibilities.

Henry Kock notes that school gardens are excellent places for learning to implement his three-part formula for restoring healthy urban ecosystems: *conservation, expansion* and *linkage. Conservation* means actively working to preserve the healthy natural areas we still have; *expansion* is a thoughtful approach to enhancing and enlarging existing natural areas; and *linkage* is the planning of new natural areas to provide connections among existing green spaces. Such linkages can encourage nature into a schoolyard from an adjoining natural area, or provide new corridors for the movement of small animals and migratory birds between previously separated patches of vegetation. Even within a small schoolyard plot, this formula shows how school gardens can become part of the Toronto region in a bigger way, connecting students to a larger part of their own place, to the wider community and to the world beyond.

Kathy Caulfield and her students at Broadacres offer an example of this kind of thinking. In their study of natural habitats, they learned that, while much attention is often paid in school to the destruction of tropical rainforests, little notice is given to the fact that 80 percent of Ontario's Carolinian forests have been cut down for development in their own part of the world. With the school's field garden and swale naturalization projects prospering, Caulfield has another naturalization project in mind. "There's some work being done now to provide flight corridors for birds that depend on the Carolinian trees. The kids have a plan for a section of the yard, by the far parking lot. They want to plant some berms and trees there in the maze area, and I'd like to put some more Carolinian trees in. We could produce a flight corridor along that side of the yard, which would give those birds a place to go during their migration."

Gardens, when seen as a part of and a connector to the surrounding world, can offer students and the community a more visceral understanding of their place in nature, of how their choices affect it, how things within it are interrelated and how people can make a difference. Viewed in this light, school butterfly gardens are far more than simply beautiful landscapes: students can stop to consider how these school-yard refuges across Ontario and indeed across Canada might become part of a migratory route for butterfly species. And students restoring part of a local ravine or valley can come to see how they contribute to the far larger and more important task of restoring water quality and health to an entire watershed.

The transformation of a piece of land, growing familiarity with the species which come to live there and the attachment that the nurturing of plants and habitats can engender help students develop a sense of caring for *their* place. Such appreciation makes a place far more alive for

FOREST VALLEY OUTDOOR EDUCATION SCHOOL
A gathering circle in the forest.

An Environmental Parable

Marsha Yamamoto, instructional leader of Toronto's Environmental Education Department, believes in the power of storytelling as a teaching tool. "I think any time you add a story to a lesson, people remember things better," she commented as she offered an environmental parable for teachers.

"We're like a little schoolhouse in the middle of a forest. And what we've done is give our students all the skills and strategies for cognitive learning and for working together co-operatively. We've given them Math strategies for problem solving and writing skills to know how to read and write and become critical thinkers. But we haven't taught them about the environment they live in. We've closed all the windows and drawn the curtains and said, 'It doesn't matter that this little schoolhouse is situated in the middle of this great forest. We don't want the kids to go outside. We have so much to teach in here.'

"And meanwhile one corner of the forest has started to burn, while we continue to work in the same way, with a 'business as usual' mentality. We never open the curtains. We never look outside. We never see the forest.

"It's one thing to do all this cognitive work, fostering the Math and Language skills and ways in which children can work together, but let's also learn about the very environment in which we live. There's a two-fold reason for students going out into the environment rather than staying inside this small, enclosed schoolhouse. One is that they can explore, connect with and apply their skills and knowledge to the very mystery and majesty of the forest we are living in. The other is that the forest is beginning to burn, and it's no longer a choice about taking the kids out: we need to take them out in that forest now and help them learn how to do something about it."